THE INCA

THE
INCA
LOST CIVILIZATIONS

KEVIN LANE

REAKTION BOOKS

To my mum and dad: LOURDES *and* JOSEPH MANUEL (PEPE)
In gratitude for literally everything
Especially for what must have seemed at times a very strange
career choice for their child

Published by Reaktion Books Ltd
Unit 32, Waterside
44–48 Wharf Road
London N1 7UX, UK

www.reaktionbooks.co.uk

First published 2022

Printed and bound in India by Replika Press Pvt. Ltd

A catalogue record for this book is available from the British Library

ISBN 978 1 78914 546 5

CONTENTS

Female figurine, 1400–1533, silver-gold alloy sculpture.

CHRONOLOGY

c. 13500 BC	First humans in the Americas
c. 12500 BC	First human occupation of South America – Monteverde, Chile
c. 11000 BC	Human colonization of the Andean mountain range
c. 8000 BC	First plant domestication in South America, among them cotton and gourd for use in nets and floats for fishing
c. 4700 BC	Oldest domesticated maize in the Central Andes
c. 4500–3150 BC	Domestication of tubers, quinoa and lupine
c. 3500 BC	Camelid domestication in the Central Andes, possibly alpaca first, and then llama
3000–1800 BC	Late Preceramic Period or Initial Period – cultural effervescence on the coast (Norte Chico) and the highlands (Kotosh Religious Tradition) based on fishing, early farming and herding

1200–200 BC	Early Horizon – rise of Chavín and related culture (Paracas, Cupisnique)
200 BC–AD 600	Early Intermediate Period – emergence of early state societies (Moche) and regional polities, including Nazca, Cajamarca and Recuay
AD 600–1000	Middle Horizon – first Andean empires, Wari and Tiahuanaco
AD 1100–1450	Late Intermediate Period – rise of coastal kingdoms (*señorios*) including Chimor and Ichma, and Balkanization of the highlands into many small chiefdoms (*curazgazos*)
1250–450	Increase in defended hilltop settlements (*pucaras*) in the highlands
1000–1200	Pre-Inca Killke phase in the Cuzco region
1200–400	Early Inca Period in the Cuzco region
1400–1532	Expansion, consolidation and collapse of the Inca Empire
1450–532	Late Horizon – apogee of the Inca Empire
1438	Pachacutec Inca Yupanqui becomes ninth *sapa* Inca (Rowe Chronology – RC); AD 1400 (Means Chronology – MC). Expands Inca Empire to northern Peru and Ecuador (Chinchaysuyu) together with generals and his heir, Topa Inca Yupanqui

1471	Death of Pachacutec Inca Yupanqui. Topa Inca Yupanqui becomes tenth *sapa* Inca (RC), AD 1448 (MC). Topa Inca Yupanqui consolidates imperial gains in the Collasuyu and Chinchaysuyu, and expands empire towards the eastern Antisuyu
1493	Death of Topa Inca Yupanqui. Huayna Cápac becomes eleventh *sapa* Inca (RC), AD 1482 (MC). Imperial consolidator, launches small-scale expansions into the eastern Antisuyu and north in the Chinchaysuyu towards present-day Colombia
1524–5	First smallpox epidemic in the Andes
1525	Death of Huayna Cápac. His designated heir, Ninan Cuyuchi, also dies, and another son, Huascar, becomes twelfth *sapa* Inca
1529–32	Inca Civil War between Huascar and Atahualpa
1532–1615	Early Spanish colonial period – 1615 coincides with Felipe Guaman Poma de Ayala's *Nueva corónica y buen gobierno* apologia to King Philip III of Spain
1532	Huascar defeated in battle, Atahualpa becomes thirteenth *sapa* Inca. Huascar is executed on Atahualpa's orders. Francisco Pizarro lands in northern Peru and proceeds to Cajamarca, captures Atahualpa

1533	Atahualpa is executed on Francisco Pizarro's orders; Túpac Hualpa becomes first Spanish puppet Inca and dies (probably poisoned by other Inca rivals) while journeying with the Spanish to Cuzco with the Spanish. Manco Inca becomes second Spanish puppet Inca
1535	Diego de Almagro sets out with Paullu Inca on a military fact-finding expedition to the Collasuyu. Manco Inca rebels against the Spanish, besieges Lima and Cuzco
1536–7	End of the First Rebellion by Manco Inca, neo-Inca state of Vilcabamba established
1537	Paullu Inca christened Cristóbal, becomes third Spanish puppet Inca
1537–9	Second Rebellion by Manco Inca, retreat to Vilcabamba
1544	Manco Inca is assassinated by Spanish rebels in Vilcabamba. His son, Sayri Túpac, becomes second Vilcabamba *sapa* Inca
1545	Silver found at Potosi
1549	Cristóbal Paullu Inca dies, last Spanish puppet Inca in Cuzco
1557	Sayri Túpac leaves Vilcabamba to live in Cuzco
1559	Mercury found at Huancavelica

1560	Sayri Túpac dies in Cuzco. Titu Cusi Yupanqui becomes third Vilcabamba *sapa* Inca
1569	Francisco de Toledo, Count of Oropesa, becomes Viceroy of Peru
1570	Titu Cusi Yupanqui dictates *History of How the Spaniards Arrived in Peru* to Martin Pando
1571	Titu Cusi Yupanqui dies. Túpac Amaru becomes fourth, and last, Vilcabamba *sapa* Inca
1572	Francisco de Toledo's troops attack Vilcabamba. Túpac Amaru defeated and executed in Cuzco
1564–72	Taqui Ongoy revivalist millennialist movement in the Central Andes
1610	Death of Melchor Carlos Inca, last legitimate grandson of Cristóbal Paullu Inca
1780–82	Indigenous rebellions in the Peruvian and Bolivian highlands under the leadership of José Gabriel Túpac Amaru, Túpac Catari, and Tomás Catari and Diego Cristóbal Condorcanqui Castro Túpac Amaru
1816	Inca Plan at the Congress of Tucumán to install an Inca as king of the United Provinces of South America, later known the United Provinces of the Río de la Plata (covering present-day Argentina, Uruguay, Bolivia and parts of Brazil, Chile and Peru)

1847	William Hickling Prescott publishes *History of the Conquest of Peru*, reviving public interest in the Inca
1911	Hiram Bingham III leads a National Geographic Society expedition to Peru. Local guide Melchor Arteaga guides him to Machu Picchu
1972	The city of Cuzco is named a UNESCO World Heritage Site
1983	Machu Picchu is a named a UNESCO World Heritage Site
2014	The Inca Road System is named a UNESCO World Heritage Site

 PREFACE

Archaeology in the Andean countries is a living science
which has to do not only with the past, but also with the
present and with the future.

PHILIP A. MEANS, *Ancient Civilizations of the Andes*

In a book series about lost civilizations we have to ask ourselves:
how lost are the Incas? The reason for this question is simple.
Many other ancient civilizations, such as Egypt, Mesopotamia
or the Indus, disappeared in the remote past, but the Inca collapsed
well within our historical timeline. The modern era is said to have
begun in the fifteenth century, with the European Renaissance and
the advent of the Age of Discovery, and definitely by 1492 when
European discovery of the Americas ushered in the first truly interconnected, globalized world, albeit one founded on colonization,
exploitation and rapine. Comparatively, the last rump state of the
Incas, that of Vilcabamba, ensconced in the lush eastern lowland
rainforest of the former empire, was finally defeated in 1572. Its last
independent ruler, Túpac Amaru, the final *sapa* Inca (Quechua for
'unique Inca'), was publicly beheaded that same year in the main
square of Cuzco – the former empire's capital – on the orders of
the Spanish viceroy Francisco de Toledo. But detailed knowledge
of the Inca Empire and its peoples lasted beyond the destruction
and chaos of the sixteenth and early seventeenth century.

The Inca Empire disappeared less than five hundred years
ago; its demise within this historical period means that direct
and indirect links to this Andean past can still be found across
many of their former lands. This is especially true of Peru and
Bolivia – areas which formed the core of the Inca dominions –
where indigenous peoples still make up more than 50 per cent
of the population, and Quechua and Aymara, two of the main
languages of the empire, are widely used. Aside from language,

Machu Picchu, citadel of the Inca.

traditions, superstitions and often worldviews harken back to the pre-European indigenous past and by association the Inca. In this volume, we analyse precisely this: evoking the Inca past, while delving into what it says about the present and future of the former imperial Inca lands, especially Peru.

Indeed, for the Peruvian state, the Inca have become a useful nationalist trope. This trope was especially helpful for at least two of Peru's twenty-first-century presidents, Alejandro Toledo (2001–6) and Ollanta Humala (2011–16). Outside of the old colonial Creole elite, these presidents found popular acclaim and legitimacy by mining their country's indigenous, and especially Inca, past. Alejandro Toledo became Peru's first indigenous president in July 2001, and was inaugurated against the imposing backdrop of Machu Picchu, that pre-eminent ancient Inca citadel and modern World Heritage Site set in the Sacred Valley, the old heart of the old Inca Empire. In so doing, President Toledo was both directly referencing his indigenous roots and stressing his government's spiritual, and indeed physical, links to the Inca Empire.

This harking back to an idealized Inca past is not a modern phenomenon. By the end of the sixteenth century early indigenous chroniclers such as Inca Garcilaso de la Vega (1539–1616) and, in particular, Felipe Guaman Poma de Ayala (*c.* 1535–1616) waxed nostalgic about the virtues of the empire and the supposed *Pax Incaica*, or Inca-imposed peace, it had brought to the conflict-ridden Andes. Later, in the eighteenth century, indigenous rebel leaders such as Julián Apaza Nina (1750–1781) and José Gabriel Condorcanqui (1738–1781) respectively adopted the titles Túpac Catari and Túpac Amaru II, both in direct reference to the last independent Inca ruler, Túpac Amaru I. Túpac Amaru II, like his ancestral namesake, was also executed in the main square of Cuzco.

Even at its more frivolously commercial or cultural level, the Inca are still omnipresent. Peru's national soft drink is known as Inca Cola, an incredibly sweet, fluorescent yellow concoction of lemon verbena or hierba luisa (*Aloysia citrodora*) and a lot of

Qulla Suyu *wiphala* flags at the National Congress Building in Buenos Aires, Argentina.

fizz. Scotland aside (Irn-Bru), Peru is the only country where Coca-Cola has not become the best-selling soft drink in the land. Rural communities and revivalist movements have ensured that the indigenous past of their countries and the culture of the Inca resonate across contemporary South American culture, from the continued existence of indigenous languages such as Aymara and Quechua, to rituals celebrating specific moments within the Inca religious calendar – for instance the *Inti Raymi* (the Inca festival of the Sun) – to a generalized veneration of the *Pachamama* (Mother Earth) across the Andean region.

Some of these cultural expressions are pure invention, with this invented material culture of the Inca being used to justify modern identity politics. A case in point is that of the supposed Inca flag – the *wiphala*. This pixelated rainbow-coloured pattern is increasingly used by indigenous groups, and others, as a sign of self-identification. In particular, the Movimiento de Unidad Plurinacional Pachakutik – Nuevo País (Pachakutik Plurinational Unity Movement– New Nation) of Ecuador uses the flag as its emblem, where the 'Pachakutik' of the title alludes to the ninth ruling Inca, Pachacutec Inca Yupanqui (1418–1472), of the traditional Cuzco dynastic lineage. Yet the *wiphala* seems to be a relatively modern invention, like the Scottish use of tartan, dating in this case most likely to the mid-twentieth century.

All these appropriations, half-truths and myths propagate the Inca ideal among local populations and governments and serve as a reminder of the past, as well as a justification for the present revindication of indigenous rights. Obviously, this happens across the world: witness the ideological tussle between Greece and the Republic of North Macedonia concerning rights over the legacy of Alexander the Great. Yet an important difference in the Andes is that descendents of the original communities are still with us today, separated by only a meagre five hundred, rather than thousands, of years from their ancestors. They live in the same areas and generate – no matter how diluted – a worldview that provides a direct link to this same past.

The question 'how lost are the Incas?' brings with it, then, a deeper query, which dwells at the heart of this book: why the

Incas? Why were they, in particular, the apex of South American civilization? What factors seem to have predestined them for glory, and how did they maintain power once they achieved it? Indeed, many beguiled travellers of the past and modern tourists alike look at the extremes of climate, altitude and landscape of the Central Andean highlands and wonder how anyone could have eked a livelihood, much less forge an empire, in these seemingly austere and harsh lands. Yet the fact remains that the same region that formed the core of the Inca Empire had previously been the location of the Wari and Tiahuanaco empires, based respectively in modern-day southern Peru and northern Bolivia, and earlier even than these, the northern Peruvian highlands were home to the widespread religious cult of Chavín. Indeed, while the coastal regions of the Central Andes were home to equally spectacular pre-Hispanic civilizations such as the Nazca, Moche and the Chimor, the area of expansive empires in the Andes was always the highlands. Coastal cultures tended to stay on the coast with only brief forays into the highlands; while alternatively, the highland Chavín, Wari, Tiahuanaco and the Inca encompassed from the coast to the tropical forests.

Travellers and tourists who see marginality and poverty in the modern Andean highlands fail to appreciate the vast underlying richness and sheer potential of this region. Its vibrancy and diversity is based on closely packed economical resources (in some areas a scant 250 kilometres (155 mi.) takes you from the Pacific Coast all the way to the Amazon) located at different ecological niches from the coast to the highlands, in intermontane valleys and onwards to the edge of the Amazonian jungle. These formed the productive backbone of the largest indigenous empire ever to grace the Americas. At its height, the Inca Empire stretched along the coast and central spine of the Andes from southern Colombia down towards Chile and northwestern Argentina, bulging eastwards towards the Amazon Basin. Home to possibly more than 15 million people, and replete with an array of cities, roads, temples, nobles, administrators and the beginnings of a professional standing army, the complexity and scale of this technologically Bronze Age empire almost defies belief.

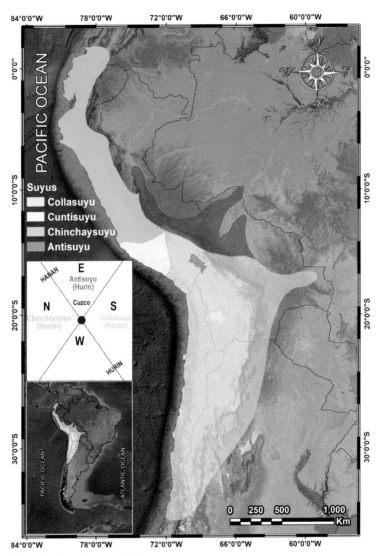

Map of the Inca Empire and its quarters.

Emerging from the Cuzco region in the southern Peruvian highlands, the Inca Empire rose to cover more than 2 million square kilometres (770,000 sq. mi.). Yet for the duration of its existence it was all but cut off from other major cultures by jungles, mountains and the South Pacific Ocean, to the extent that the Incas, and indeed South American civilization, emerged – similarly to

Mesoamerica – largely independently of outside influence, thereby developing a distinct South American worldview and manner of doing things. The peculiarities of the Incas extended, for instance, from their 'writing' based on knots on strings known as *quipu*, to an almost complete lack of a trading currency, and a highly animistic local and state-based religion.

In this book, then, we explore the development of Inca culture, society and economy within the ecological and geographical context of South America, and how by the fifteenth century their empire rose to dominate western South America. We focus on their myths, history and beliefs, and how, even after collapse, their memory inspired generations from the sixteenth century to the twenty-first century. Finally, we reflect on their continued influence: an influence that still matters for many across the Andean region.

ONE

TAHUANTINSUYU: LAND OF THE INCAS

> What I summarize is that, the continuation of the land of
> the Indies with those others of the world, at least those
> which are closest, has been the most important and truest
> reason for the settlement of the Indies . . .
>
> JOSÉ DE ACOSTA, Historia Natural y
Moral de Indias (1590)

'Tahuantinsuyu' was the Inca name for their kingdom, comprising four separate regions – Chinchaysuyu (North), Antisuyu (East), Collasuyu (South) and Cuntinsuyu (West) – with the capital, Cuzco, at its centre. The name pivots on the infix *-ntin*, meaning something that is 'intimately bound together', rendering the translation something along the lines of 'land of the four intimately connected quarters'.

The Inca kings, lords of the Tahuantinsuyu, were the last rulers of a wholly indigenous state to emerge in the Andean region before the arrival of the Spanish in AD 1532. Although rumours of a new *El Dorado* or 'city of gold' had existed following the earlier Conquest of Mexico (1519–21), it would be another ten years before Europeans reached the Andes. What the Europeans found in the region amazed them, from its wealth to the size of its human population and the technologies those inhabitants used. With more than 10,000 years of nearly independent cultural development, the Andean region constituted one of a rare number of 'cradles of humanity', where the rise of civilization had been wholly autochthonous. This was an honour shared only with Egypt, Mesopotamia, India, China, Mexico and possibly Western Africa. So unique was this civilization that the late anthropologist and ethnohistorian John V. Murra (1916–2006) coined the expression *lo Andino* – the Andean – to explain what he saw as an intrinsically Andean way of thinking, making and doing.

Millennia of near isolation, then, had forged a very distinct civilization, conditioned by its unique ecology and environment. This chapter will present the people before the Inca, and their environment and economy, by briefly charting the development of Andean civilization from the peopling of the continent to the emergence of the eponymous empire. Here we dwell on the particularities of the Andes, from the extreme diversity of its environments – a compact east to west transect, the South Pacific Ocean, coastal deserts, lush riverine and intermontane valleys, high-altitude tundra and jungles – to the accompanying richness of its ecology. For instance, roughly two-thirds of the world's amphibians are endemic to South America, as are one-third of its birds, almost half of all reptiles and one-third of our planet's fish.

To better understand the Inca, then, we must delve into that past and engage with the setting that allowed them to become the pinnacle of South American power by the mid- to late fifteenth century. As the Jesuit scholar José de Acosta (1539–1600) correctly surmised in the epigraph to this chapter – and more than a hundred years before European reconnoitre of the Bering Strait by the homologous Danish explorer Vitus Jonassen Bering (1681–1741) – initial human colonization of the Americas was began from the continent of Asia, then moving across what is now the Bering Sea, into Alaska and then into the larger American land mass. Recent genetic studies suggest that the indigenous populations of the Americas were directly descended from East Asian populations that had experienced some earlier ancient Eurasian gene flow. These people moved eastwards and then southwards across this new continent.

The generally accepted earliest dates for human settlement of the Americas suggest this event occurred around 15,500 years ago, during the last Glacial Maximum (24,500–12,500 BC), when the Bering Strait would have provided a land bridge known in scholarly literature as Beringia. Multiple theories as to how this original peopling of the Americas occurred coalesce around two main routes of colonization: the first being big-game hunter-gatherers travelling through an ice-free corridor between twin glaciers in northern North America; the second, the maritime route of fisher-gatherers, who followed shoals of fish and marine mammals southwards along the Pacific Coast. What is also certain is that they brought domesticated dogs with them for use in hunting, and possibly for food. Initial colonization of South America was probably instigated by these fisher-hunter coast-hugging groups, their presence most fully evidenced by sites such as Monteverde in southern Chile, dated to around 12,500 BC. From these inauspicious beginnings, humans rapidly populated the rest of the continent of South America, with inhabitation of the high Andes commencing around 11,000 years ago. Once settlements on the Andean mountain range appeared, humans had colonized almost the full range of Andean habitats. Recent tentative gene flow evidence of later Pacific peoples (around AD 1200) might indicate that pre-Hispanic South America was not always as isolated as earlier studies may have assumed.

Traditionally, using a mixture of indigenous terms and ecological classifications, the central Andean region has been divided into eight separate ecological zones from west to east: coast/*chala*, *yunga*, *quechua*, *suni*, *puna*, *jalka*, upper forest (*rupa-rupa*) and lower forest (*omagua*) – these last two serving as precursors to the Amazon. The coast/*chala* (at an altitude between 0–500 metres (up to 1,640 ft) combines the rich Pacific Coast fisheries with the

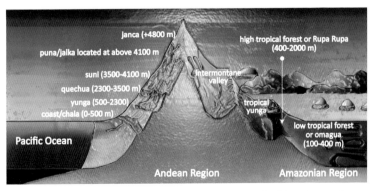

Central Andean ecozones, after Javier Pulgar Vidal, *Geografía del Perú: Las ocho regiones naturales* (1967).

equally productive fluvial floodplain created by the strong rivers and streams whose waters come from the Andean mountain range. This coastal area is narrow and surrounding this reduced area of productivity lies a dry, severe shrub-and-sand desert with low hills (*lomas*), which flower annually due to the prevalence of moisture-laden sea fog, known as *garúa*. In addition to its maritime resources, this area would have been ideal for the cultivation of early domesticates such as cotton, gourd, squash and maize, alongside later domesticated plants including fruits, vegetables and pulses.

Further inland, the subtropical and humid *yunga* is located at an altitude of between 500 and 2,300 metres (1,640–7,550 ft) and occurs at two separate locations in the Andes: just above the immediate coastal region (coastal *yunga*), and to the east, where it borders with the upper tropical forest (riverine *yunga*). A singularly productive zone, this is the main area for coca cultivation (*Erythroxylum coca*) and for the production of myriad varieties of fruits and vegetables, including maize and sweet potato, as well as chilli peppers. Above the *yunga* comes the *quechua* (2,300–3,500 metres (1,640–11,500 ft) above sea level). This is the main, and altitudinally, last major, agricultural zone in the highlands, important for beans, maize and potato agriculture. The potato (*Solanum tuberosum*) is a mainstay of highland diets and was crucial in ensuring the sustenance of highland – and Central Andean – civilization. Further up in the Andes comes the *suni/jalka* ecozone at between 3,500–4,100 metres (7,550–13,450 ft) above sea level. This represents the transitional mixed-economy area between the agricultural *quechua* and the pastoralist alpine tundra (*puna*) that characterizes the highest productive agricultural zone of the Andes. In the suni and jalka ecozones, agriculture is increasingly difficult given the high temperature fluctuations and ground frost, making this a landscape of short stunted trees and meagre shrub cover. Nevertheless, hardy crops do grow at this altitude, including bitter potato, quinoa, cañihua, tarhui, oca and olluco.

The *puna*, located at above 4,100 m up to the snowline, effectively represents the last productive ecological zone. An area of night frosts and extreme diurnal temperature fluctuations, not much grows in this zone aside from short, tough grasses, which serve as the dietary basis for the animals that inhabit this austere landscape. Before the Spanish conquest (AD 1532), the *puna* was traditionally the area for camelid (alpaca and llama) herding and for the hunting of their wild primogenitors (guanaco and vicuña). Cold and harsh though this zone might be, it was the main animal-rearing area of the Andes. Camelids were a crucial resource of the pre-Hispanic Andes and essential to the emergence and subsistence of Andean civilization. The highland empires of the Andes – Wari, Tiahuanaco, Inca – owed their expansionist achievements to the power of the camelid, especially the llama and its function as a pack animal. Nowadays the introduction of European animals has meant a drastic decrease in the number of native camelids, with the area also being used for rearing goats, sheep, cattle, horses and donkeys. Above the *puna* come the glacial peaks of the Andes: vast expanses of snow and ice that cap the Central Andean cordillera. The Central Andes are comprised of three mountain ranges: one bordering the Pacific Coast, a central range comprising the spine of this mountain chain and a further one along the edge of the Amazon jungle. Of these, only the central one is substantially glaciated.

Further to the east lie the last two recognized ecozones of the Central Andes, the upper (*rupa-rupa*) and lower forest (*omagua*). Essentially the beginning of the Amazon, these zones comprise a dense, humid cloud forest teeming with exotic flora and fauna. Although pre-Hispanic Andean cultures interacted with this forest zone, there seems to have been little permanent penetration or colonization of these areas by highland groups – the Incas included. Across this diverse environmental setting, the compressed nature of this ecological archipelago is striking. In northern Peru, the distance between the coast and the jungle is a meagre 250 kilometres (nearly 125 mi.), while at its widest, around Lake Titicaca in the south, it is barely double that, at most.

While the Inca were a Central Andean people, the culture nevertheless expanded, both north towards modern-day Colombia and south to Argentina and Chile. Essentially, the map of the Inca Empire follows the boundary of the pre-Hispanic maize agricultural frontier and, more importantly, the maximum range of then existing llama pastoralism. Although we will deal with this in more detail later, it is important to note that the llama was the main beast of burden of the pre-Hispanic Andes, and therefore an essential tool in the expansion of the Inca Empire. North and south of the Central Andes, the eight ecozones described above vary somewhat. Towards the north the *puna* peters out, turning into *páramo* in Ecuador and Colombia. The *páramo* is a cold, humid ecozone of low productivity, but high and varied floral density. It also represented an inhospitable barrier to pre-Hispanic camelid pastoralism and therefore probably Inca expansion into it.

To the south the *puna* undergoes dramatic changes, becoming increasingly drier and lower in altitude as the Andes stretch away from the tropics, such that in northwest Argentina the *puna* is located in the region above 3,200 metres (10,500 ft). As the Andes become wider towards the south, the areas of *puna* also become larger and more contiguous, creating a series of altiplanos – high-altitude plains – the most important of which is located around Lake Titicaca, straddling the modern borders of Bolivia and Peru. The desert *puna* of southern Bolivia, northern Chile and northwestern Argentina present bleak and austere landscapes of stunted shrub-lands and meagre plant cover, yet they provided the setting for large pre-Hispanic camelid caravans and successful mixed agricultural and pastoralist economies.

Although humans had colonized the gamut of these ecological zones by around 11000 BC, the first stirrings of plant domestication occurred much later (*c.* 8000 BC), along the Pacific Coast and Amazonian tropical forest, especially the *yunga* ecozone in both areas. In particular a focus of emergent civilization was the area known as the Norte Chico, covering the coast/*chala* ecozone of the Supe, Huara, Pativilca and Fortaleza valleys. Here we have the emergence of the first complex societies, with monumental architecture and compact residential areas. Perhaps the most impressive of these early sites is that of the inland settlement of Caral, which covers a 66-hectare (164 ac) area and includes plazas, sunken circular ceremonial structures and seven terraced pyramids or platform mounds.

Platform mounds of Caral-Supe, Peru.

Significantly, these early sites (3000–1200 BC) – especially those along the coast, such as Aspero, Bandurria and Huaricanga, among others – did not contain any ceramic, seen in many parts of the world such as the Near East as an essential storage component for plant domestication. Rather, these sites seem to have concentrated their economy on the exploitation of the rich marine resources of the Pacific Coast. This led archaeologist Michael Moseley to propose his 'maritime hypothesis' in 1975 for the development of Andean civilization, whereby early social complexity was based on the successful capture and consumption of vast quantities of maritime products. Although this theory has now been partially discredited – a more nuanced view has the simultaneous devel-opment of both coastal and inland sites through a combination of fishing and agriculture – fishing of this exceptionally rich marine

zone, mainly for anchovies, sardines and shellfish, would have provided the impetus for the domestication of cotton (*Gossypium barbadense*) for use in nets and possibly gourd (*Lagenaria siceraria*) for use as floats and containers. Archaeological remains of both cotton and gourd suggest that they were domesticated along the Pacific Coast area with early evidence for them in the Gulf of Guayaquil and the north-central Peruvian coast, respectively. Alongside these utilitarian domesticates, we have evidence of the early agriculture of squash, pulses, chilli peppers and fruits such as guava, avocado and lucuma, and lowland tubers including sweet potato. Taken together, all these products provided the wherewithal for the successful emergence of social complexity and civilization along the Pacific coast.

In the highlands the march towards civilization initially went at a different pace. The contemporary Kotosh Religious Tradition (essentially a religious architectural style, 3000–1800 BC) of the north-central Andes was a lesser affair, featuring small self-contained buildings with niches and a central hearth ventilated by horizontal flues. These ventilated rooms had their analogues on the coast, suggesting that the highlands at this time were engaged in a set of beliefs and rituals that they held in common with coastal sites such as Caral (Supe Valley), La Galgada (Santa Valley) and Huaynuná (Casma Valley), among others.

Interestingly, these first stirrings of organized religion in the highlands occurred coevally with camelid domestication further south. Domesticated South American camelids – llama and alpaca – seem to have emerged in the south-central Andean highlands by around 3500–3000 BC in the Junín and Ayacucho areas, although it is possible that independent centres of llama domestication occurred in northwest Argentina and northern Chile at the same time. During the pre-Hispanic period, these camelids and their wild cousins – guanaco and vicuña – represented, alongside deer, the prime meat-protein element of South American diets. It is possible that animal domestication in the Andean highlands happened in symbiosis with plant domestication, leading to the cultivation of tubers, quinoa and lupine together with that of camelids around 4500–3150 BC.

With plant and animal domestication throughout the Central Andes, the stage was set for further cultural development during the so-called Initial Period (3000–1200 BC). From the Initial Period we start getting into the chronology of periods and horizons. These were the hallmark of John Rowe (1918–2004) and his students. Rowe was a pre-eminent Andean scholar and Incaologist, whose excavation and ceramic seriation of the Ica Valley provided the basis on which to map all subsequent Central Andean timelines. Based mainly on ceramic forms and ceramic art style, Rowe's chronology harked methodologically back to the classical culture–historical timelines elaborated for Old World civilizations, such as that of Egypt. Although not without its flaws, this chronology has stood the test of time, with even the advent of radiometric dating (for instance radiocarbon dating) unable to dislodge it from its position as a tool for understanding cultural and societal shifts in the Andean past.

With Rowe in tow, beginning with the Initial Period, we have a series of three initial or intermediate periods and three horizons – Initial Period, Early Horizon, Early Intermediate Period, Middle Horizon, Late Intermediate Period and, finally, the Late Horizon. In simple terms, the Initial and Intermediate Periods were moments of cultural effervescence and heterogeneity, while Horizons represent the consolidation and expansion of more homogenous stylistic forms across the Andes. While the Initial and Intermediate Periods encompass a diversity of styles and cultures, Horizons underpin the rise of larger cosmological or political movements, such as Chavín (Early Horizon), Wari and Tiahuanaco (Middle Horizon), and finally the Inca (Late Horizon). Interestingly, all three Horizons describe highland phenomena, and underscore the seemingly intrinsic expansionary impetus of the Andean highlands throughout South American prehistory.

The Initial Period is characterized by deepening social and economic developments along the coast and highlands, leading to the widespread use of canal-irrigated agriculture, ceramic production and early textile weaving that used both cotton and camelid fibres. Important sites attributed to this period abound both on the coast and in the highlands, from Caballo Muerto in the coastal Moche Valley, to Chiripa on the Titicaca Basin. The generalized social, economic and cosmological development of these diverse Initial Period cultures was the harbinger of the first pan-Central Andean cultural manifestation, that of Chavín, and with it the Early Horizon (1200–200 BC).

The site of Chavín de Huántar is located in north-central Peru, on the eastern flanks of the Cordillera Blanca – part of the central glaciated cordillera of the Andes – set roughly 3,150 metres (2 mi.) above sea level and located along an important transit corridor that connects the eastern rainforest to the Andean highlands and onwards to the coast. Sprawling and monumental, Chavín de Huántar is a multi-layered religious site with a series of internal galleries, multiple temples, subterranean water canals (possibly employed as acoustic props in ritual ceremonies), plazas, elaborately carved stelae and panels, and anthropomorphic tenon heads in various stages of transformation, suggestive of the transmogrification associated with imbuing psychedelic substances. These substances most likely included the mescaline-based San Pedro cactus (*Echinopsis pachanoi*), which appears in Chavín iconography. Construction of this temple site was organic, in so far as it presents continuous alterations and modifications to its core structure. Indeed, this is a common feature of many Andean temple constructions and has been seen at Caral and, later on, in Moche (Huaca de la Luna and Huaca del Sol) and Nazca (Cahuachi) architecture.

Given his detailed description of a site very similar to Chavín, it is possible that when the Discalced Carmelite monk Fray Antonio Vázquez de Espinoza (1570–1630) travelled through the area in 1616, he witnessed the worship of a godlike figure known as Guari. Guari was the agricultural deity of a large region of the north-central Andes from the Late Intermediate to early Colonial Period (AD 1000–1615). At the time, this would have made Chavín de Huántar the longest continually used religious site in South America. Indeed, the Lanzón de Chavín, a 4.5-metre (15 ft) granite stela (its shape is reminiscent of the *chaquitaclla*, the Andean foot plough) engraved with mixed bird-like, feline-featured carvings, located in an underground gallery at the heart of the Old Temple, is probably the oldest *in situ* religious object in the world. In the Andes, these types of object were known, and are still referred to, as a *huanca* or a sacred stone.

While two of Peru's fathers of archaeology, Julio C. Tello (1880–1947) and Rafael Larco Hoyle (1901–1966), disputed, respectively, whether the origins of Chavín were highland or coastal in nature, neither argued the significance of Chavín for the Central Andes. Its art – depicting felines, caimans, anacondas and taloned, fanged birds, among other real or mythical beasts – was found in different guises, but in similar style, all the way from the Piura Valley in the north to the Nazca Valley in the south, covering an equally broad swathe of the highlands. Julio C. Tello thought that the site's pivotal position between the cordillera and the Amazon meant it served as a conduit for trade and the transmission of ideas from east to west. Be that as it may, for many scholars Chavín's lack of overtly military or monarchical iconography suggests that it may have functioned as the all-important pilgrimage and oracular centre

Temple of Chavín, Peru.

of a religious movement that swept the Central Andes for some eight hundred years. Interestingly, the Chavín culture's image of a 'staff-god', that of an individual holding a staff in each hand, crops up later on in many different guises, across a variety of cultures, especially that of the Middle Horizon Tiahuanaco. The image was even used by the Inca, for whom it seems to have represented different things in different places, including Viracocha – the Inca supreme creator deity – the Sun, the Moon and the god of rain, thunder and lightning, known variously as Illapa, Thunupa or Libiac, depending on the region of the Andes.

The disappearance of the Chavín culture ushered in the Early Intermediate Period (200 BC–AD 600) and with it a period of increased cultural divergence across the Andes. It was also a time when the coast once again overtook the highlands in political and economic complexity. Warrior iconography across many of the representative cultures of this period – Moche, Nazca, Recuay, Cajamarca and Huarpa, among others – attests to a period of greater instability and internecine warfare. The Moche (AD 250–850), centred in the northern valleys between the Piura and

Nepeña rivers, rose as a series of interrelated, highly structured, valley-based, hierarchical state societies, based on political control through the deification of leaders, elaborate rituals and a penchant for sacrifice and bloodletting – these last activities possibly being entered into as a means to assuage elemental forces such as the recurrent El Niño phenomenon. The El Niño–Southern Oscillation (ENSO) phenomenon is an extreme warm water event that develops in the central and east-central equatorial Pacific, affecting the Pacific Coast of South America with unseasonal floods on the coast and drought in the highlands.

The sumptuous tombs of the Moche, such as those of the Lord of Sipán, Lady of Cao and the Priestesses of San José de Moro, attest to the power and prestige of these royal and religious elites, as do their temple pyramids, known as *huacas*, such as the Huaca del Sol and Huaca de la Luna (Sun and Moon temples) in the Moche Valley. Exerting tight economic and ideological control over these river valleys, the Moche established relations with cultures such as the Cajamarca and Chachapoyas in the northern highlands, and Recuay in the north-central highlands, as well as with Vicus on the far north coast and the Lima culture along the central coast.

Further to the south, the Early Horizon coastal Chavín-influenced Paracas culture (700 BC–AD 1) gave way to the Early Intermediate Period Nazca (AD 1–700). Architects of the enigmatic Nazca Lines, a series of elaborate geoglyphs on the dry pampas and hills of the Río Grande de Nazca Valley, the people of the Nazca culture flourished in the valleys bounded by the Cañete and Acarí Rivers, along a coastal strip more than 375 kilometres (233 mi.) in length. Like the Moche, direct control and influence over the highland hinterland was limited. Much less politically organized than the Moche, the Nazca coalesced around small hamlets, with society organized by spiritual shamans and petty chiefs sharing regional commonalities in religious belief and lifestyle. While rank attained through a lifetime of service seems to have defined honour and prestige within Nazca society, rather than class predetermined at birth, the constant imagery of warfare in pottery, as well as weapons and trophy heads found in burials, shows that this was also a highly developed warrior society. Practitioners of skull modification and early skull surgery known as trepanation, the Nazca were also excellent textile weavers and potters, creating some of the most distinctive and emotive art of the ancient pre-Hispanic world. It seems that Nazca art and style influenced that of the neighbouring highland Huarpa culture: the direct precursor to the Wari Empire, a behemoth of the subsequent Middle Horizon (AD 600–1000).

Although the Middle Horizon, the second of these homogenizing stages, is essentially seen as a Central Andean phenomenon, its reverberations spread well beyond the confines of the Wari and Tiahuanaco empires to northwest Argentina, in the form of La Aguada (AD 600–900), and possibly to Ecuador, through the Manteño culture (c. AD 600–1600). Such was the influence

Reconstruction of the royal tomb of the Lord of Sipán, Lambayeque, Peru.

and reach of these two empires that one could easily speak of a Middle Horizon Renaissance in the Andes, in which a unified social, political, economic and cosmological project ensured imperial success. With this, there was a new power shift from the coast to the highlands. Initially, during the first half of the twentieth century, scholars thought that Wari and Tiahuanaco were two sides of the same coin, with Wari representing the coastal and northern expression of the more southerly Lake Titicaca and Altiplano-centred Tiahuanaco. It was the pioneering work of researchers in the 1950s, such as the doyen of Andean prehistory Wendell C. Bennett, Arthur Posnansky and the inimitable John Rowe, followed by other notable modern-day archaeologists such as William H. Isbell, John Janusek, Alan Kolata, Gordon F. McEwan and C. Ponce Sanginés, that began disentangling the cultures from each other. Together these researchers reached the

Double-spout vessel, Nazca culture, Peru, c. 6th–7th century AD, with trophy heads hanging at the waist.

conclusion that, while there are considerable iconographic similarities between Wari and Tiahuanaco art, especially in the use of staff-god imagery – a prime example being the Gate of the Sun at Tiahuanaco's eponymous capital – they were two very different types of states.

The Wari, with their similarly named capital near the modern town of Ayacucho in the central Andes, seem to have been the heart of a much more structured empire than that of Tiahuanaco. A number of similarly designed Wari administrative centres such as Pikillacta, Huaro and Viracochapampa scattered across more than 1,000 kilometres (620 mi.) served as the unifying thread for a complex system of regional, direct and indirect rule of such diverse areas as the northern highlands and central Andean coast. These centres were probably interconnected by a network of state-maintained roads. On the other hand, the Tiahuanaco seems to have concentrated its monumental sites within a radius of no more than 75 kilometres (46 mi.) around their central capital of the same name, Tiahuanaco. Scholars have suggested that Tiahuanaco expansion southwards through modern-day Bolivia, Chile and Argentina was more the effects of their camelid caravan trade and influence rather than out and out conquest, perhaps interspersed by a number of far-flung colonies. In this sense, the spread of Tiahuanaco culture was similar in character to that of the earlier Chavín Horizon. Like Chavín, the site of Tiahuanaco comprised a series of temples, semi-subterranean plazas and a plethora of carved stone art, much of it referencing the staff-god, such as the Gateway of the Sun and the Ponce Monolith. These similarities have led some scholars to suggest that the site of Tiahuanaco served as the oracular pilgrimage centre of a widespread highland cult. Nevertheless, signs of military tension along the frontier between these two states in the southern Peruvian coastal Moquegua Valley demonstrate that peaceful coexistence between these two very different empires was not necessarily a given.

The Middle Horizon is important as it represents the last expansive state moment in the highlands prior to the Incas. As such, the Middle Horizon was the inspiration for a number of later components integral to Inca statecraft. The Inca likely adopted roads from the Wari as an essential strategy used to bind the sinews of the empire together, along with standardized administrative centres and the organizational support that propped the empire. They also probably incorporated the *quipu* – a mnemonic knotted-string system used for record-keeping and for encoding more complex narratives. Inca adoption of Lake Titicaca as their place of origin, coupled with its transcendent importance in their myths and legends, led to a new Inca-sanctioned sacralization of the lake and its surroundings. This included the construction of important temples on the Islands of the Sun and Moon, and gift-giving offerings to the lake. The Inca also incorporated Tiahuanaco as a sacred site within their cosmological landscape. This meant that the old Tiahuanaco imperial homeland ended up representing the *urheimat*, or origin, of the Inca, with all that meant for legitimacy of the Inca state and their rulers. It is also possible that the first language spoken by the Inca was Puquina, which likely had its origin around Lake Titicaca and has been mooted as the language spoken by the ancient Tiahuanaco people. Tiahuanaco's seemingly more indirect form of control of its territories also presaged Inca strategies across large parts of the empire, especially in their expansion southwards into Chile and Argentina.

Yet the true legacy of the highland-based Middle Horizon is the symbiosis and specialization created around agriculture based on three products – maize, potato and camelids. The economy based on these products went hand in hand with the wholesale development and technological advances in hydraulic architectural construction undertaken by the Wari and Tiahuanaco people, especially of terraces, raised field systems and irrigation canals. Although these technologies had a long pedigree in the Andes, it was during the Middle Horizon that they were combined into one powerful highland economic package. In this sense, much more than with the earlier Chavín Horizon, the Wari and Tiahuanaco empires unlocked the key to prosperity in the high Andean region, turning an ecologically rich, though underexploited, region into a veritable breadbasket that ably served their needs. Later on during the fourteenth and fifteenth century, it would essentially be this

Ponce Monolith, Bolivia.

economic model that would underpin the expansion of the Inca Empire. As with all empires, both Tiahuanaco and Wari eventually collapsed, the victims of political hubris, over-expansion, and possibly of adverse climatic conditions. In their wake a multitude of smaller entities emerged, heralding the start of the Late Intermediate Period (AD 1000–1450), and with it the rise of the nascent Inca.

Although a definitive grasp of Andean prehistory is made difficult by a lack of historical sources, by the Late Intermediate Period we have our first glimpses of this hidden, unwritten past. The rapidity of Inca conquest and the relatively short time span between this and Spanish colonization meant that a certain degree of historical memory pertaining to this earlier period still existed when the Europeans arrived – a historical memory gleaned from interviews that the early Spanish chroniclers used for their historical narratives of this newly colonized and subjugated land. This means that the image we have of this more recent past – as usually happens in history and archaeology – is more complete and, perforce, complex.

Returning to the archaeology, the denouement of the Wari and Tiahuanaco empires precipitated a severe fragmentation of the Andes, what some scholars have called a 'Balkanization' of the region. While this process was felt across the whole of the Central Andes, it was much more acute in the highlands. Along the coast, a series of larger political entities, including the kingdoms of Ichma and Chimor, among others, contrasted with the heavily divided nature of the highlands. Chimor, or Chimú as it is known in archaeology, in particular was a highly advanced and consolidated state that ruled in, and beyond, the old Moche cultural area, eventually bringing into its fold all the coastal valleys between the Chira in the north and the Huarmey in the south. Its capital at Chan Chan, in the Moche Valley, was the largest adobe city in the Americas (19 sq. km, or 7 sq. mi), and from here a well-developed state oversaw and organized the kingdom.

Like other earlier and coeval coastal groups, the Chimor did not extend overmuch into the highlands, although ethnohistoric documents show that they maintained reciprocal trade relations and alliances with groups further inland. Indeed, in the eventual conflict for hegemony between Chimor and the Inca, the former could call on the help of these neighbouring highland groups. Nevertheless, resistance failed when the Incas defeated them through battle and siege, leading to the dismantling of their kingdom. The fate of Ichma along the Central Peruvian Coast was somewhat different. Although much less politically organized than the Chimor, the Ichma kingdom housed within its confines the powerful oracle of Pachacamac. This oracle's importance transcended that of the Ichma kingdom, such that it was a pilgrimage centre for peoples across the Central Andes. Effectively, the Inca assimilated Pachacamac and its cult into the imperial pantheon by appending a massive temple of the Sun and elevating this site, together with Lake Titicaca, as an important centre for the godly creation of humankind, and, by association, the Inca.

In turn the highlands presented a very different picture, with a large number of small polities engaged in widespread raiding, warfare and internecine violence. The Late Intermediate Period in the highlands can be divided into two unequal segments, an earlier one between AD 1000 and AD 1250, where population increased but violence seems to have been more restrained, followed by the period after AD 1250, in which defended high-altitude hilltop settlements – known generically as *pucaras* – were built to safeguard an increasingly threatened population. It seems likely that, in certain parts of the Andes – especially the Cuzco area from where the Inca emerged – it took the first two and a half centuries of this period for political power to coalesce into more complex forms, making the second half of the Late Intermediate Period one in which these different petty chiefdoms fought for control.

Needless to say, the pattern was more complex than this simple summary, and there was much local variation (the old Wari heartland of Ayacucho, for instance, actually became less complex with the onset of the Late Intermediate Period). In general, however, the Late Intermediate Period and endemic conflict presaged a general altitudinal shift upwards by the people in these regions, with populations increasingly hugging walled enclosures among the inaccessible peaks and ridges of the Andes. Such a move likely precipitated an expansion of camelid herding during this period, aided by a cooler, drier climate that would have greatly increased the amount of grassland available. Interestingly, this highland fragmentation into small kin-based groups occurred all the way from Ecuador through to northwest Argentina. Incidentally, the expansion of viable camelid herding during this period followed the rough contours of the later Inca Empire across the Andes.

Cast adrift from centralized centres of power throughout this period, these smaller petty chiefdoms probably practised a much looser form of political power in which social stratification was low and leadership was mostly non-hereditary. Especially during the early period, leaders probably emerged as and when they were necessary. In the absence of strong leadership, social cohesion was guaranteed by kinship and ancestor worship. Although veneration of dead ancestors seems to have been a long-standing tradition in the Andes, it took on new import during the Late Intermediate Period with the strategic placing of funerary towers and tombs on the boundaries of territories or alongside economically important areas in their lands. Beyond the purely strategic or economic, ancestor worship was a means of maintaining and renewing ties among the larger family, village or kin-group. Among this plethora of Late Intermediate Period groups were the Killke, named after a style of ceramic, of the Cuzco region. It is from these humble beginnings that we can trace the emergence of the Inca as the pre-eminent empire of the Andes.

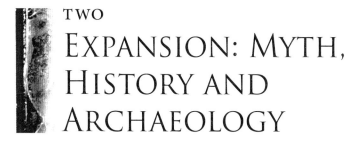

TWO

EXPANSION: MYTH, HISTORY AND ARCHAEOLOGY

They did not count their age in years; neither did they measure the duration of their acts in years; nor did they have any fixed points in time from which to measure historical events, as we count from the birth of our Lord Jesus Christ.

FATHER BERNABÉ COBO, *History of the Inca Empire* (1653)

The Inca are unique in being the only ancient empire never to develop or adopt a written script, although they did utilize the *quipu*, from the Quechua for 'knot': knotted string arrangements that were used to record administrative data, and also functioned as mnemonic devices for encoding larger narratives. Although some of these *quipu* narratives were transcribed during the early Spanish colony from cord-keeper (or *quipucamayoc*) witnesses, the majority of what we know about the Inca's more remote past was gleaned by Spaniards or *mestizos* (mixed Spanish–indigenous South American parentage) from interviews with indigenous informers. This lack of indigenous script, coupled with an oral storytelling tradition and a non-linear method of recording calendrical dates, means that this Inca past is inevitably jumbled, obscure and open to multiple interpretations. To compound the issue, the earliest interviewers – those physically closest to the pre-Hispanic past – were themselves Spanish. These Spanish chroniclers rarely spoke the indigenous language, usually had a poor grasp of the social, cultural and religious concepts underpinning Inca and Andean society, and came with their own agenda and deeply held precepts and prejudices.

For instance, Pedro Sarmiento de Gamboa (1530/32–1592) interviewed more than a hundred members of Inca nobility for his impressive *History of the Incas* or *Historia Indica* (1572), including *quipocamayocs*. While the final work is both detailed and informative, we must consider, however, that Sarmiento de Gamboa had been hired by the Spanish Crown to discredit the Inca and their conquests, presenting them as tyrants and thereby justifying subsequent Spanish conquest and suzerainty of their empire. Overt agendas like this were hardly conducive to an unbiased appraisal of Inca myth and history. Likewise, the Inca witnesses had their own interests and agendas, with most of them favouring their own households, known as *panacas*, and kin. Most definitely, modern historians or anthropologists they were not.

Nevertheless, sifting through often contradictory accounts of the Inca past, a pattern emerges, and it is this pattern that we can contrast against the archaeology to better define the rise of the Inca. In this chapter we trace the mythical and the probable ethnogenesis of the Inca, their rulers and their physical expansion, drawing on ethnohistoric sources, historical interpretation and archaeological data to tease out a coherent narrative charting the rise of the Tahuantinsuyu during the Late Intermediate Period (AD 1000–1450) through to the Late Horizon (AD 1450–1532). But even this is laced with contradiction, so we therefore provide two possible models of Inca expansion. The traditional model, proposed by John Rowe, has the Inca Empire expanding rapidly, first to the centre and north, and then south, beginning in 1438 and culminating in 1532 with Spanish conquest and colonialism. A second model initially proposed by Philip Ainsworth Means (1892–1944), and then supported by modern radiocarbon dating, argues for a slower, earlier expansion, beginning towards the end of the fourteenth century, initially to the south and then north. We will assess these two different interpretations below.

Turning to the origin of the Inca, we find the creator-deity Viracocha, who created humankind at Lake Titicaca. These original humans were sent through underground routes, eventually emerging from sacred places – *pacarina* – in the landscape, providing origin points for the various peoples across the land. Sometime later, the same Viracocha and his two sons crossed the Andes, calling these people forth to propagate and populate the land. This central concept of the *pacarina* (and wider religious precepts) was a commonality that the Inca shared with other Late Intermediate Period cultures. The nascent Inca therefore believed in the mythical *pacarina* – place of origin – where people would have emerged, fully formed, in a single moment of community genesis. A *pacarina* could be a cave, a lake, a spring or any prominent feature in the landscape. In the case of the Inca, this was a cave named Pacarictambo, or 'Tavern of the Dawn', located some 26 kilometres (16 mi.) southwest of Cuzco (although some Inca hagiography contends that each of the Tahuantinsuyu quarters or sectors had its own Pacarictambo, thereby setting the Inca as having originated everywhere in the subsequent empire).

To complicate the matter further, there was also a hierarchy to the concept of *pacarinas*, from the more local, and therefore of lesser importance and associated to kin-groups, to regional ones linked to people (such as the Inca) and then pan-regional *pacarinas* that provided the origin point for large swathes of Andeankind. One such case is that of Titicaca Lake, which for the Inca was the birthplace of their creator-deity, Viracocha. Even so, Lake Titicaca was one of the most important central *pacarinas* of the highland for a variety of groups, among them the Inca. Indeed, by the Late Horizon, the Inca had identified two such pan-regional origin places: one in the highlands, Lake Titicaca, associated to Viracocha, and another on the coast, the Pacific Ocean associated to Pachacamac and his great oracular temple site on the coast. Yet the conceptual development of these two ultimate *pacarinas* was a late one, and likely a product of Inca imperial political hegemony. In this sense, the Inca strove to subsume all other Andean *pacarinas* under these two imperially sanctioned places of human origin. In so doing, the Inca were instigating what countless other civilizations have done: integrating, usurping or supplanting local religious belief under a ruler's religion.

While we will deal with Inca cosmology in more detail later, suffice to say that the theme of two places for the origin of the Inca – Lake Titicaca and Pacarictambo – served two different imperial purposes. While the Lake Titicaca origin myth became the proxy for explaining the formation of the Andean world by the Inca creator-god Viracocha, justifying Inca pre-eminence and their right to rule. Similarly, this Inca connection to Lake Titicaca served to link the Inca with the foregone grandeur of the Middle Horizon Tiahuanaco present in their eponymous ruins. On the other hand, the Pacarictambo myth is much more intimate and proximal, involving the 'birthing' of the first *sapa* (unique) Inca: Ayar Manco, later known as Manco Capac, his sister/wife Mama Ocllo, and three brothers with accompanying sister/wives: Ayar Auca/Mama Huaco; Ayar Cachi/Mama Ipacura or Cura; and Ayar Ucho/Mama Raua.

The best accounts of the Pacarictambo myth are related in the chronicles of the above-mentioned Pedro Sarmiento de Gamboa and his compatriot Juan Diez de Betanzos (1510–1576). This latter conquistador married an Inca princess, Cuxirimay Ocllo, mistress of Francisco Pizarro (the leader of the Spanish military expedition against the Inca in AD 1532) and wife of former Inca Atahualpa (1497/1500–1533). Cuxirimay Ocllo was later baptised and renamed Angelina Yupanqui. As an Inca princess, Cuxirimay Ocllo, or Angelica Yupanqui, was related to Atahualpa's father, *sapa* Inca Huayna Cápac (*c*. 1467–1525). Juan Diez de Betanzos learnt Quechua and through his high-status wife had privileged access to high-ranking Inca informants and sources such as royal *quipu* even if these belonged to one particular household, or Pachacutec's Hatun *panaca*, his wife's household.

To return to the Pacarictambo myth, the eight Inca founders emerged from a set of three caves known as Tambo Toco (meaning 'the house of openings', located at Pacarictambo). These three caves were called, from left to right, Maras Toco, Capac Toco and Sutic Toco. From Maras and Sutic Toco emerged the Maras and Tambos (Sutic) populations, key early allies of the Inca. Out from the central opening – Capac Toco – came the eight Inca founders, dressed in fine woollen clothes and gold adornments. There is some argument about whether the emerging pairs were siblings or husband and wife, although considering Inca rulers penchant for marrying their sisters, half-sisters and first cousins, it is perhaps a moot question. It is also worth considering that these women, as either sisters or wives, or both, were given leading roles in the creation myth, underscoring the importance of women and matriarchy within Inca, and highland Andean, pre-Hispanic society. Scholars have also noted that the prefix 'Ayar' comes from the Quechua word for 'corpse'. Thus, with the use of 'Ayar' in these founding members of Inca ancestry, they were establishing from their mythological onset the connection between the living and the dead, in this case mummified ancestors or Inca hereditary rulers, much in the same way as other cultures across the Central Andes were doing.

Together with their allies, the Tambos, these founding fathers and mothers of the Inca nation wandered northwest, in search of land to settle. As they went, they tested the earth with a golden rod looking for fertile soil. Along the way they faced various trials and tribulations, such as the birth of the second Inca, Sinchi Roca, son of Ayar Manco and Mama Ocllo. Later on, Ayar Cachi, the rowdiest and most violent of the brothers, was tricked into returning to Tambo Toco for some objects that had been left behind. Once he did, the rest of the group sealed the cave behind him. Next, the remaining seven siblings arrived at Huanacauri mountain, situated near Cuzco. From here they discerned the Cuzco Valley for the first time. Thrusting the gold rod into the ground, the Inca saw that it disappeared, proving that the area was rich, fertile and therefore a propitious place for their new homeland. It was at Huanacauri that another of the brothers, Ayar Ucho, turned to stone after conversing with the Sun and changing the first-emerging Paucarictambo brother Ayar Manco into Manco Capac (supreme one), duly consecrating him as the first *sapa* Inca. Ayar Ucho's stone idol was key to an important Inca shrine located at Huanacauri.

From Huanacauri the Inca proceeded to Cuzco, where they were welcomed by the local leader, Alcaviça. Alcaviça, believing them to be direct descendants of the Sun, allowed them to settle in the valley. Once settled, Mama Huaco introduced maize to the valley. Ayar Auca, the final brother left, transformed himself into a stone pillar, leaving the path open for Sinchi Roca to become *sapa* Inca after Manco Capac. With Ayar Auca out of the picture we have the erstwhile ruler, his son and his four sisters to claim Cuzco for the Inca. Naturally, this story is both self-serving and mythical. Nevertheless, as Sir Arthur Evans discovered with Knossos and the minotaur, or Heinrich Schliemann with Helen of Troy, at the heart of many myths lies a small kernel of truth.

Recent DNA studies on descendants of Inca rulers living in Cuzco cautiously suggest that the patrilineal line of the individuals tested originated in the Lake Titicaca area, just like the Inca founding myth suggests. A more generalized DNA study presented in Izumi Shimada's recent book entitled *The Inka Empire* (2015) explains that the Cuzco basin DNA mainly belongs to the Altiplano/Titicaca Lake group, giving credence to the idea of a southern Peruvian highland origin to the Inca. Although dating when this DNA was first present in this area is difficult, tentatively this is gauged at some point in the last 1,000 years – exactly during the turbulent Late Intermediate Period, for which we have substantial evidence for the movement of people across large areas of the Andean highlands. These movements of people were often the basis for enduring local myths, such as that of the settled *Huari* farmers and the wandering *Llacuaz* herders of the central and northern highlands (the latter dislodging the former from positions of power, similar to the wandering Inca dislodging the settled people under Alcaviça). Indeed, the theme of strong herders versus weaker farmers is a recurrent one and belies the importance that herding had for Late Intermediate Period Andean highland society as a whole – an importance that was later reflected under the Inca with their llama caravans, herds and massive investment in camelid fibre production.

The linguistic evidence is also suggestive of a Titicaca Lake origin for the Inca. Cuzco, the core of the Inca Empire, was at the crossroads of three major highland languages: Aymara, Puquina and Quechua. Today only Aymara and Quechua are spoken in the Central Andes. Puquina was already in decline by the sixteenth century and had disappeared completely by the nineteenth century. Yet at its peak the language extended over a large area of southern Peru, Bolivia and northern Chile. Centred around Lake Titicaca, Puquina was eventually displaced by Aymara in its heartland, although it might have served as the language of the Middle Horizon Tiahuanaco Empire (AD 600–1000). Even though the root of the place name 'Cuzco' is Aymara, the modern Peruvian palaeolinguist Rodolfo Cerrón-Palomino has eloquently defended the case for Puquina being the so-called 'secret language' of the Inca, with Aymara being the lingua franca of the early period of the empire before Quechua become the mainstay during their expansion northwards. This still leaves Puquina, with its circum-Titicaca Basin origin, as the possible precursor language to both Aymara and Quechua in the region.

One further strand of evidence concerns ceramic style. Tantalizingly, the similarities between imperial Inca and earlier Lake Titicaca ceramic points to a possible stylistic influence coming from the Titicaca region northwards into the Cuzco area at a time before the emergence of a fully fledged Imperial Inca style of pottery.

Although the myths, DNA, language and ceramic evidence are but tentative strands of a fragmentary history, taken together it does suggest that the Inca most likely had their origins in the melting pot of cultures and groups of southern Peru and northern Bolivia, maybe even the Lake Titicaca area, establishing themselves early on in the Cuzco Valley. More prosaically, the archaeology points to a slow consolidation of power by a number of pre-Inca groups such as the Antasayas, Ayarmaca, Mohina, Pinagua and Tambo, among others. Importantly, these groups shared a type of ceramic known as Killke, or Killke-derived, which would later evolve into the Inca style. While the spread of a ceramic style or material culture does not necessarily indicate political control, it can delineate emergent embryonic hegemony by the instigator group, in which their wares and products are seen by the groups adopting them as providing local prestige and status.

Unfortunately, much of the pre-Inca archaeology in the core area has been overlain by later Inca building, such that teasing an accurate history of this area during this period is difficult.

Nevertheless, the archaeology posits that the population in the Cuzco area increased with the demise of the Middle Horizon Wari (AD 600–1000); indeed the collapse of Wari as a political entity did not lead to an accompanying decline in the area's population. In fact, the Cuzco area was known for its continuation and new establishment of further open settlements by predominantly low-valley maize farmers. Open, undefended settlements present a very different pattern to what we would expect from the politically Balkanized Late Intermediate Period (AD 1000–1450) and points to an early consolidation of power by a Cuzco proto-urban elite. It was this early establishment of power that probably gave the Incas the drop on neighbouring groups allowing them to further amass territory and authority on their subsequent precipitate ascension to empire.

The transition from the Killke to the early Inca period is set at around AD 1300, by which time the Inca would have had a vastly more consolidated power base than their neighbours, a huge advantage for the wars of conquest to come after AD 1400. Yet the Inca were but another one of the many small groups vying for power in the cauldron of the Late Intermediate Period politics, and their king list reflects a desire to achieve legitimacy by establishing, at least in their personal history, a long ancestry and therefore hold on the land.

To take the list compiled by Miguel Cabello Balboa (1530/35–1608), an early Spanish chronicler writing in his *Miscelánea Antártica*, it is clear that after the Inca founder – Manco Capac – we have another ten Inca rulers, before the brothers Huascar and Atahualpa and the subsequent Inca Civil War (1529–32), just prior to the arrival of the Spanish:

Manco Capac
Sinchi Roca
Lloque Yupanqui
Mayta Cápac
Cápac Yupanqui
Inca Roca
Yahuar Huacac

Royal Inca aribalo or *urpu*.

Killke ceramic, Muyumarca, Cuzco, Peru.

Miniature aribalos or *urpus* from San Jacinto, Pamparomas, Ancash.

Viracocha Inca
Pachacutec Inca Yupanqui
Topa Inca Yupanqui
Huayna Cápac

Most Inca scholars see little historicity in this king list. Indeed, Andean researchers such as Catherine Julien point out that the very idea of a king list was an attempt to link it to the established Spanish king list, and thus render Inca history understandable to the new colonizing power post-1532. The mythologizing inherent to the Inca list of kings can also be seen in the claims that some of the earlier rulers governed for more than a hundred years, as well as in their actions, which in many cases were magical and extraordinary. For instance, Inca Roca – the sixth Inca – averted drought in Cuzco by plunging his hand into the earth where he could hear water running, and subsequently bringing it forth.

Therefore, most academics tend to acknowledge perhaps the last four or five rulers (from either Inca Roca or Yahuar Huacac) as historical figures; some go so far as to consider only the last three – Pachacutec Inca Yupanqui, Topa Inca Yupanqui and Huayna Cápac – as bona fide verifiable. Yet what can be agreed upon, both from the archaeology and the ethnohistory of the area, is that the Inca emerged from the Cuzco Valley towards AD 1000, and through slow, incremental development reached a significant level of cultural, architectural and organizational complexity by the mid- to late fourteenth century: the necessary precursor to successful expansion.

In this sense, we can discard the wilder speculations of Felipe Guaman Poma de Ayala, who records an Inca dynastic list covering more than 1,500 years, or that of Fernando de Montesinos (c. 1593–c. 1655), who in the early seventeenth century compiled a table of 93 pre-Inca kings, attempting to link the Inca to the deep past of South American antiquity. Lest we forget, however, Fernando de Montesinos also ascribed a Lake Titicaca origin to the Inca – very much in keeping with recent Inca scholarship. Even so, alongside the enduring lack of clarity concerning the origins and life history of the early Inca, we have a much deeper, more relevant problem with Inca chronology, namely that of the length of time it took for the empire to expand.

As it stands, most of the early Spanish chroniclers agree on an Inca timeline that spans between 350 to 450 years. Furthermore, ethnohistoric consensus generally agrees that the Inca coalesced around the Cuzco area during the eleventh and twelfth centuries. This is not the timeline of empire, however. The path to empire apparently pivots around the Chanca Wars, for all intents and purposes a liminal event in Inca hegemony over the Andes. The supposed Chanca Confederation was a group of tribes to the north and west of Cuzco, in the old Wari heartland, that united and presented the most formidable of foes to the fledgling Incas. Most, but importantly not all, chroniclers agree that this occurred in the time of Pachacutec Inca Yupanqui, immediately before his accession to the throne.

In this story Pachacutec is not the heir to the throne; his brother Inca Urcon is. Inca Urcon is their father's –Viracocha Inca – favourite and heir designate. Yet when the Chanca advance towards Cuzco both Viracocha Inca and Inca Urcon flee the coming battle. With the Incas in dire straits, the Inca creator-deity Viracocha himself (or the Sun, in other accounts) appears to Pachacutec, rousing him to resist the Chanca and promising aid for his cause. In a surprise reversal of fortune, Pachacutec rallies the Incas around Cuzco and with the aid of Viracocha, who transformed stones into warriors (known as *pururaucas*), completely routs the Chanca and forces their submission. Two other Chanca armies are also defeated in quick succession, leading to a total Inca victory.

When Pachacutec presents the spoils of war to his father, Viracocha Inca, they are spurned, leading the young man to eventually defy him, setting himself up as *sapa* Inca and reordering Cuzco and its environs. It is only later, with Urcon Inca conveniently out of the picture, that Viracocha Inca returns to the capital to bestow the royal fringe (*mascaipacha*, the Inca symbol of royalty) on his victorious son. With the Chancas defeated the imperial dream can finally be realized, with expansion and conquest radiating out from the capital to encompass most of western South America.

Nevertheless, the historicity of the Chanca Wars is much disputed. Recent archaeological fieldwork by Brian Bauer and his team in the Chanca heartland has proven that the Chanca were nowhere near as organized or powerful as the Inca made them out to be. Cuzco was four times larger than any place found in the Chanca area; given this, and other particulars, it seems highly unlikely that the Chanca could have provided any measure of sustained threat to the nascent Inca Empire. More importantly, if you remove the fantastical frills of this tale, Pachacutec's ascent over his father and brother reads very much like a palace coup, justified by a grasp for power through the pretext of a Damoclean existential threat.

This was not a rare occurrence with the Inca. Primogeniture as a system of kingly succession was not an established modus operandi for them, and the death or marginalization of a ruling Inca could lead to multiple would-be heirs vying for the throne. Situations like these were not helped by the fact that a ruling Inca had multiple wives, and hence many children. By way of example, after the Spanish garrotted Atahualpa in 1533, they installed, in short order, three puppet Incas, all of which were sons of Huayna Cápac (Atahualpa's father) through different mothers. In the Inca past neither the ascension of Topa Inca Yupanqui nor Huayna Cápac was peaceful, and they both had to lead wars of reconquest against rebellious provinces and to subjugate potential rivals, most of them close kin. The Inca Civil War between the brothers Atahualpa in Quito and Huascar in Cuzco, at the empire's end (1529–32), was yet another extreme example of this.

And so, on to the knotty problem of dates for Inca expansion and rule. The actual chronology of the Inca kings remains disputed. Until now the most widely accepted dates have been those presented by Miguel Cabello Balboa, as interpreted by John Rowe in the mid-twentieth century. Rowe dismissed most of the early kings as fictional and concentrated on the last three, providing actual dates for their accession to the Inca throne, with Pachacutec Inca Yupanqui in 1438, Topa Inca Yupanqui in 1471, and Huayna Cápac in 1493. This led John Rowe to propose his fast-expanding empire model, in which these three individuals were the effective face of the Inca Empire, heralding the moment that the imperial state came into being. With Huascar ascending to the throne upon the death of his father, Huayna Cápac, in 1525, and Atahualpa usurping it in 1532 on the eve of the Spanish conquest of the Inca Empire, this theory would suggest that the empire lasted for a mere 108 years.

In Rowe's narrative, eight fictional early ruling Inca brings their 'history' down to the all-important ninth sovereign, Pachacutec

Inca Yupanqui, who, with his defeat of neighbouring tribes during the Chanca Wars, initiates the empire's expansion. The 'Pachacutec' in the name was an autonym given on ascending the throne, meaning 'he who transforms the world'. In this narrative, Pachacutec Inca Yupanqui could well be viewed as the South American equivalent of Genghis Khan, whose vision and aggression ensured Inca hegemony over the Andes. If John Rowe and his reading of the Spanish chroniclers is to be believed, in less than a hundred years Pachacutec, his son Topa Inca Yupanqui and grandson Huayna Cápac had quite literally created the empire. A subsequent civil war between two of Huayna Cápac's sons, Huascar and Atahualpa, culminated with Francisco Pizarro capturing the victor, Atahualpa, and imposing Spanish rule on this Andean Empire. Since Rowe first proposed his chronology, in 1945, this version of events has been chapter and verse, yet as archaeology and radiocarbon dating have progressed, the date of 1438 for the start of Inca expansion has come into some dispute.

Indeed, building on the ideas of previous scholars (such as Terry D'Altroy, Veronica Williams, Virgilio Schiappacasse and Anna Adamska) a new generation of Inca researchers across the different regions of the erstwhile empire – such as Alan Covey in the Inca heartland, Dennis Ogburn in Ecuador, Martti Pärsinnen in Bolivia and Argentina, Catriel Greco and Erik Marsh in Argentina and Luis Cornejo in Chile, among others – are fleshing out a chronology based on recalibrated radiometric dates. Be it radiocarbon dating on organic remains or thermoluminescence on ceramics, the new dates for the southern half of the empire, the Central Andes and Ecuador are starting to push the chronology of Inca expansion back to the late fourteenth and early fifteenth centuries, or even earlier in some cases. This opens the possibility of an empire that lasted 150 years or longer, rather than a blitz of less than a hundred years.

We should note that while the normal error margins of a single date cannot invalidate the traditional Rowe chronology, it is rather the ever-growing body of dates available that are shifting the parameters of what we would regard as the expansion of the empire. Tantalizingly, this dating evidence suggests that expansion was initially to the south, through northern Chile and then northwestern Argentina, before a later expansion north, with Ecuador incorporated into the empire at least twenty years earlier than Rowe is suggesting.

This more gradualist model has the Inca expanding first to the south and then northwards. Interestingly, this model was presaged in a now seemingly obsolete book by Philip Ainsworth Means entitled *Ancient Civilizations of the Andes*, published in 1931. Means, from his reading of Inca Garcilaso de la Vega's important *Royal Commentaries of the Incas*, proposed an initial contained Inca expansion commencing in the thirteenth century. While these extremely early dates would seem to be somewhat fanciful, it does make for remarkably interesting reading, especially in the light of the new dates we have pertaining to expansion of the Inca Empire. Indeed, Inca Garcilaso de la Vega posits the ascent to empire starting with the eighth Inca, Viracoca Inca – Pachacutec's father, rather than Pachacutec himself. This discrepancy could well be down to the identity of this particular chronicler.

Inca Garcilaso de la Vega was a *mestizo* son of a Spanish conquistador and an Inca princess, and therefore well placed to garner information concerning the rise of the Inca. Yet he was also a scion, through his mother, of the lineage of Topa Inca Yupanqui (the tenth Inca), inveterate enemies of the descendants of Pachacutec Inca Yupanqui's household. This may well have clouded Inca Garcilaso's narrative, as the Peruvian ethnohistorian María Rostworowski de Diez Canseco (1915–2016) has so cogently argued. Therefore, Philip Ainsworth Means's foundation for the historical Inca section of his book, based entirely on Inca Garcilaso de la Vega, does open it up to criticism – although in light of new archaeological evidence it would be good to revisit some of Means's grander themes and ideas concerning Inca expansion. Ironically, Philip Ainsworth Means died a year before John Rowe published his treatise on Inca chronology, which largely discredited Means's then in-vogue gradualist model. Indeed, the ability of powerful academics to underwrite and establish a dominant paradigm is not without precedent (witness, for instance, the ongoing controversy surrounding the early peopling of the Americas between Tom Dillehay and his detractors, or concerning the domestication

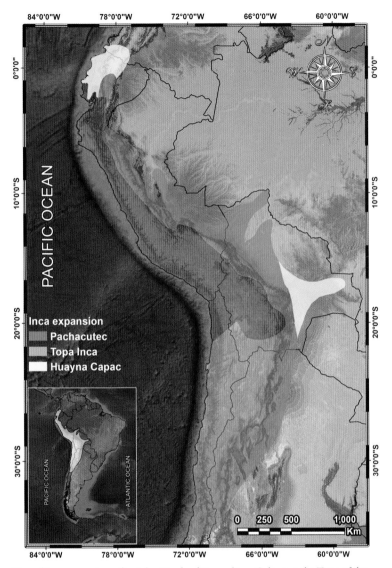

84°0'0"W 78°0'0"W 72°0'0"W 66°0'0"W 60°0'0"W

0°0'0"

10°0'0"S

PACIFIC OCEAN

20°0'0"S

Inca expansion
Pachacutec
Topa Inca
Huayna Capac

30°0'0"S

PACIFIC OCEAN   ATLANTIC OCEAN

0 250 500 1,000
Km

84°0'0"W 78°0'0"W 72°0'0"W 66°0'0"W 60°0'0"W

Map of Inca expansion, after John Howland Rowe, 'Inca Culture at the Time of the Spanish Conquest' (1946).

of maize between those proposing a single origin to maize in Mesoamerica, such as Dolores Piperno and Deborah Pearsall, and those advocating multiple points of origin, for instance Alexander Grobman and Duccio Bonavia). The Inca imperial blitz model has been assiduously defended by Rowe and his followers.

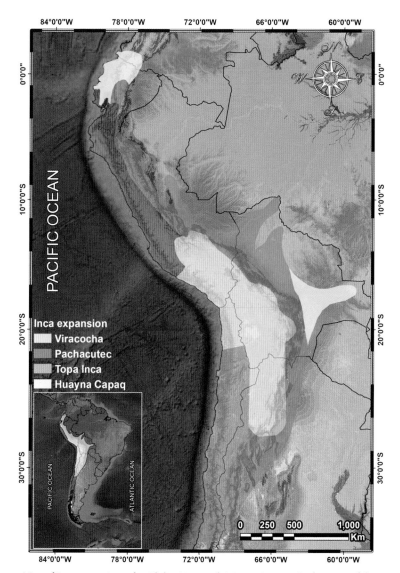

Map of Inca expansion, after Philip Ainsworth Means, *Ancient Civilizations of the Andes* (1931).

Yet it now seems that the gradualist model is making a slow, though sustained, comeback. A common feature to both models is the inexorable advance of the Inca Empire and the importance of Pachacutec Inca Yupanqui to the narrative of this expansion. Even with Inca Garcilaso rooting for Viracocha Inca as the conqueror of the Chanca, both in Means's and Rowe's retellings, Pachacutec remains the man under whom the first serious push for empire occurs. Emerging radiometric chronologies also argue for an earlier expansion that first headed south.

In keeping with his earlier dates for expansion, Means sets Pachacutec's reign from 1400 to 1448, rather than Rowe's 1438 to 1471. Subsequently, Topa Inca Yupanqui would have reigned between 1448 and 1482, rather than Rowe's 1471 to 1493. Finally, under Means, Huayna Cápac would have reigned from 1482 to 1525, rather than Rowe's 1493 to 1525. In disentangling this narrative, the dates for Huayna Cápac are very interesting. Scholars agree that Huayna Cápac was born around 1467, and that he was still young when he became Inca – young enough for his early reign to have been marked by a regency under two of his uncles, Gualpaya and Guaman Achachi. If we follow Rowe's date for Huayna Cápac's ascendency then he would have been around 26 – hardly an innocent youth – while under Means's alternative chronology he would have been around fifteen years old, a much more plausible age for a brief regency. One final point to consider is the meaning of Huayna Cápac's name in Quechua, which is 'young ruler'.

In considering the length of the Inca Empire, one could wonder whether these extra few decades are significant. I would have to say yes, since it would allow the Inca more time to consolidate themselves across the Andes. It would also explain the vast amount of infrastructure that they were able to build throughout the empire. While a century and a half might seem a short time for such an overarching empire, we should consider that the 'Second' British Empire (after the loss of what became the United States) lasted between 1783 and 1950, only slightly more than 150 years. This amount of time gives the state administrators, whom royal myths of conquest would not bother mentioning, enough time to adapt to local situations. Multiple generations of local groups would have to interact with imperial agents and comply with their rules, backed up, if need be, by force. For instance, the southern half of the empire, with its seemingly endless high-altitude grasslands and llamas, might have initially attracted the Inca, given the llama's pivotal importance in transporting goods and wares for trade, especially during wartime. Later on, silver, gold and other minerals might have provided the impetus for the empire in these far-flung southern regions. Also, given the sparseness of southern populations in comparison with those to the north, the south might just have been easier to conquer than the substantial, well-organized northern territories. The kingdom of Chimor on the northern Peruvian coast, as well as the populous regions of Huaylas, Cajamarca and modern-day Ecuador, would have been difficult adversaries for the Inca.

An initial Inca expansion south before the north would also go some way towards explaining the inconsistency in languages spoken by the Inca. Linguists have long argued that the dominant language in the Cuzco Valley during the Killke and early Inca Period would have been Aymara. At the time, the main Aymara-speaking area would have been from Cuzco to the south. This might in some way justify why Inca expansion was towards the south first, where their common language – Aymara – was spoken. Aymara place name toponyms have been found throughout the highlands of southern Peru, Bolivia and into northern Chile and Argentina, perhaps suggesting early Inca control of the area. Only in the early to mid-fifteenth century, when the Inca moved north into the populous Quechua-speaking areas, does Quechua then become lingua franca of the Cuzco area and the empire.

Returning to the vexed issue of Inca expansion, while Rowe's chronology still largely holds sway in modern research circles, there is enough evidence – both ethnohistorical and archaeological – to start seriously positing a different interpretation in terms of expansion and concerning the regnant period of the individual *sapa* Incas. Thus, while in this book I generally use Rowe's dates for the individual *sapa* Inca reigns, I do consider the arguments set above as a clarion call to re-examine the complex nature of the chronology of Inca expansion and the individual regnant periods.

By the mid-fifteenth century, imperial expansion led to the Inca subjugating a vast number of tribes, statelets and kingdoms, possibly spanning from the Maule River in southern Chile to the modern border between Ecuador and Colombia. To the east, the

Inca rarely extended beyond the Andean foothills, and the deep Amazon forest and the pampas of Argentina provided an insurmountable obstacle to their expansion, a physical as well as an economic obstacle. The Inca economy was irretrievably linked to Central Andean agriculture and camelid herding. In this sense, the eastern as well as the northern and southern borders of the empire had stretched to a maximum of the then limits of viable Central Andean agriculture and llama herding.

The limits of the empire by the beginning of the sixteenth century were therefore probably dictated as much by the administrative and logistical shortcomings of what was essentially a Bronze Age civilization, as by the frontiers of this Central Andean economy. This is not to say that beyond the Inca frontier farming did not exist, just that it was of a type unfamiliar to the Inca. Indeed, one could say that the Inca conquered the known world in a similar manner to, say, the Roman Empire of the Antonine dynasty (AD 96–192), which reached its self-professed maximum extent, delimited by what they understood of the then known world. So, as with every empire, we have to distinguish between its real frontier and that liminal zone in which imperial influence vied with independent local persistence. Therefore, while it might have been possible for the Inca to expand into the Argentina pampa, or into the extreme south of Chile, there might have been no inclination to do so, as the populational base was too low, or the distances to and from the more central areas of the potential empire too vast, to make it necessary or feasible. We can justifiably say that, as with the Romans, by the beginning of the sixteenth century the Inca had conquered all the 'known world' – or at least as much of that world as they deemed it necessary to invest in.

Aside from the hyperbolic Chanca, the Inca did face strong resistance during their expansion, none more so than the Chimor kingdom ensconced in the fertile valleys of coastal North Peru. While other groups and cultures were coerced through a mix of threats and incentives, the Chimor were eventually comprehensively defeated by the Inca, serving as an example of the reach and might of this last Andean empire. Once defeated they came under the Inca in a form of clientage whereby the Chimor lords continued their rule under the tutelage of the Inca. On the cusp of European contact, the Inca Empire covered a large area of western South America, coalescing a vast number of different people and cultures stretching from the northern tropics of Ecuador and Colombia, to Chile and the saltpans of northwest Argentina, and eastwards to the edge of the Amazon forest. A truly remarkable achievement, considering the limits of essentially Bronze Age technology.

THREE

AUTHORITY, RELIGION AND IDEOLOGY

The Indians of Peru were so idolatrous that they
worshipped as Gods almost every kind of thing created.
FATHER BERNABÉ COBO, *Inca Religion
and Customs* (1653)

How to rule an empire? Under the Incas, ultimate power lay with the *sapa* Inca (the unique Inca), a descendant of the Sun and a virtual god-in-being. In an age when the separation of religion and state across the world was non-existent, being a living god ensured that religious, social, political and economic authority ultimately rested on the Inca himself, in much the same way as in feudal Europe it had lain with supposedly god-anointed monarchs sanctioned by the clergy.

However, given the size of the Inca state it would have been impossible for the Inca to personally control the minutiae of the empire, and as such they relied on a well-organized and oiled machinery of state that percolated from the capital and the Inca godhead to the provinces and villages throughout the empire. Inca rule was an admixture of both direct and indirect forms of government, and although most local people would rarely have seen an 'Inca' in the flesh, so to speak, their power encompassed all the nooks and crannies of the empire. In this sense, it is important to highlight that few people would have actually been 'Inca'; most would have been allied parties that maintained their local identities and ascribed to Inca imperial ideals. In fact, the lineage of the Inca was much reduced, and although this was expanded in time through recourse to the elevation of certain personages to 'Inca-hood', their numbers always remained low in respect to the empire's overall population.

In this chapter we will delve into how religion formed the basis around which to legitimize the Inca state – the state ideology – while also providing a link to long-lasting Andean traditions embedded in ancestor worship and animism. In so doing we will analyse how the empire was managed by close kin of the Inca and organized into ancestral households, known as *panacas*, which were then overseen by Inca nobles, conquered local leaders who had been elevated to the position of honorary Incas, or Incas-by-privilege, and cadres of local administrators. It is first important to understand Inca religion and where it came from, however. It is crucial to realize that large sections of Inca religion – and, by extension, ideology – were not innovations; rather, the Inca were the culmination of hundreds of years of religious development in the Andean highlands. While certain aspects of Inca religion were probably new, such as the Sun cult of the empire, the main underlying aspects of their belief system had its roots in Andean animist traditions, especially highland ones.

A number of issues arise in any consideration of a past culture's religion. This is especially so in the case of the Andes, where no writing existed from the indigenous perspective at the moment of Spanish contact; *quipu*, a mnemonic 'writing' device on knotted strings, seems to have been unsuitable for long, elaborate narratives, rather coding short messages and tabulating amounts. The ethnohistoric accounts of Andean folklore, apart from some notable exceptions such as the *mestizo* and later indigenous chroniclers, were written by Spaniards usually on official engagements, such as tribute or tabulation *visitas* or officials engaged in the eradication of 'heathen' practices through the *Extirpación de Idolatrías*. Furthermore, the indigenous writers of mixed birth, or *mestizos*, born just after the Spanish conquest, were already somewhat removed from the events and rituals that they describe. Inca Garcilaso de la Vega, for instance, was writing at the end of his life, having left the Andes for Spain almost fifty years previously; he also wrote a highly partisan account. This bias arose from the fact that these learned *mestizo* chroniclers usually belonged to one or other of the Inca *panacas*, and thus embellished the accounts of their household and forefathers. In Garcilaso's case this meant that he unduly praised the deeds of his *panaca*, that of Túpac Inca Yupanqui, the tenth Inca and his ancestor.

The Spanish accounts, such as those of Juan de Betanzos, Sarmiento de Gamboa, Cieza de León and Bernabé Cobo, similarly suffer from the prejudices and biases inherent to early colonial narratives. Many of these early authors did not know or understand what it was that they were describing; others pandered to a certain viewpoint or perspective that would have been welcomed or expected back in Spain. Sarmiento de Gamboa, for instance, was assigned by the authorities to investigate and discredit Inca claims to long-term suzerainty of large swathes of the Andean region. Nevertheless, for all their problems, early documentary sources remain a crucial tool for disentangling the intricate web of indigenous beliefs. This is particularly true of the set of documents produced as a consequence of the *Extirpación de Idolatrías*. Known as the bastard child of the Spanish Inquisition, the *Extirpación de Idolatrías* collected and collated indigenous accounts of ritual practices and religion.

In sum, while all these accounts – indigenous, *mestizo*, Creole and Spanish – present invaluable insights into the pre-Hispanic worldview underpinning Inca religion and politics in the Andes, they are flawed and must be taken with a veritable pinch of salt. An additional important source is the work undertaken by eminent ethnohistorians such as María Rostworowski de Diez Canseco, Gerald Taylor, Peter Gose, Pierre Duviols and especially R. Tom Zuidema on this matter. Their critical assessment of ethnohistoric sources adds context and meaning to these documents and are integral to elucidating past Andean belief systems, economy, society and politics.

In so far as religion is concerned, three main themes permeated Andean highland and Inca beliefs: animism, oracular divination and ancestor worship. For a long time, animism was seen as synonymous with primitive religions, but more recently it has been interpreted as a way that certain peoples understood their world without the added appendage of it being more primitive or advanced. As such animism is understood as the interaction or relatedness between people and animals, or environments, emphasizing the real or imagined life force that animates them. In animistic religions, the 'gods', spirits or manifestations inhabit, and are represented actively in, the world around them – a veritable holistic living-in-the-world. In this sense, animism opposes the separation that exists between the physical and the metaphysical in many Western religions, such as Christianity.

In the animistic Andes, indigenous communities were an essential component of the living and lived-in environment and landscape; effectively, the whole world was alive and intimately interrelated. In many ways one could call it a 'religion of space', emphasizing the truly enveloping nature and reach of Andean religion. Even so, within this landscape approach to religion and animism there were aspects of the world that were more 'alive' than others: what the indigenous people termed *camac* from the Quechua root 'to animate', otherwise interpreted as 'aliveness'. In an Andean world full of *camac*, the main wellsprings of this aliveness were *huacas*, and especially their ability to 'talk' and, crucially, to engage in oracular divination. While in the Andes all nature was animated, or potentially animated, a *huaca* was a particular spirit or deity revealed as an object, feature or even natural occurrence. These included such items as mummy bundles (dead ancestors wrapped in woven textiles), trees and naturally occurring free-standing rocks or outcrops, as well as mountains, hills, rivers, springs and all manner of other physical manifestations, including rain, hail, lightning, thunder and wind.

Veneration of these deities and spirits was widespread and conducted in sanctuaries, temples, mortuary monuments and natural locations such as lakes, spring heads and caves. All these locations were also known collectively as *huacas*. An effigy or idol was a common personification of a *huaca*, especially if this was of something that was impossible to venerate physically, such as lightning or thunder. Obviously, the term *huaca* also covered their representations, as they would be imbued with the spirits' essence. These idols came in many shapes and sizes, from carved

Camelid conopa, 1470–1532, stone sculpture.

Bean pod *conopa* from Yurakpecho, Pamparomas, Ancash, Peru.

stone, wood, dough, ashes or precious minerals, to common rocks and stones (for instance, as *conopas* or *illas* – miniature carved representations of crops or animals). The concept of *camac* underscored the principal characteristic of a *huaca*, and through that the *huaca*'s ability to impart oracular wisdom. Indeed, the more powerful the *huaca*, concomitantly the more *camac* it had, and the greater the potential truth of its oracular prophecies or predestinations. *Camac* was a constantly shifting essence, therefore the relationship between people, *huacas* and the wider animated environment was complex and in constant flux. Interaction with these physical manifestations of Andean – and Inca – animism had to be constantly renegotiated through libation, offerings, consultation, worship or even violence, which could mean a *huaca* being a friend, kin or an outright enemy.

The power of a *huaca* derived directly from oracular pre-destination, its strength from the veracity of their divinations. Therefore, a *huaca*'s power could wax and wane depending on how this ability manifested itself. Conquered people's *huacas* became subservient to the main *huaca* of the conqueror, so much so that the Incas would haul these provincial oracles back to Cuzco as spiritual hostages. In turn this allowed for the realignment of these *huacas* within the Cuzquenian ideology as well as subordinating them under the central Inca cult. When the *huacas* were eventually returned to their places of origin they helped perpetuate the ascendency of the imperial cult. Another particularly powerful expression of *huaca* and wider ideological subjugation can be seen in the *capacocha* ceremonies, where children from the provinces were sacrificed to, and by, the Inca. These children were selected by regional dignatories and would visit Cuzco with their *huacas* before being sacrificed as a ritual of affirmation of Inca power, forging a link between their homeland and the imperial capital. This ritual was also a forum whereby provincial *huacas* could negotiate with the principal Inca *huacas* residing in Cuzco.

One type of *capacocha* required children to be sacrificed on mountain summits, as seen with the Llullaillaco mummies found in Salta, Argentina. This type of sacrifice was particularly prevalent in the southern half of the empire. *Capacochas* could be undertaken for a variety of reasons, including prior to Inca armies marching out to battle. In a society underscored by ties of reciprocity, the *capacocha* was the ultimate gift-giving token between a ruler, or his representative, and the gods.

In assimilating human characteristics, *huacas* lived and died. So, while *huacas* functioned as a source of wisdom and information, they could also disappear entirely. Indeed, the number of *huacas* became so large that the eleventh Inca, Huayna Cápac (AD 1493–1525), sought to rationalize the system of *huacas* by declaring war against them and actually ridding the Inca Empire of a large number of them. The thirteenth Inca, Atahualpa (AD 1532–1533), also destroyed the Central Andean *huaca* oracle of Catequil

Silver god-effigy figure wrapped in textiles and feather headdress found with *capacocha* sacrifice at Llullaillaco, Argentina.

because it had predicted that his brother Huascar would win the civil war that raged between them. Similarly, Atahualpa also destroyed Topa Inca's body (the tenth Inca, AD 1471–93, itself a *huaca* oracle), his attendants and as many of his descendants as he could lay his hands on, due to this *huaca*'s support for Huascar.

Andean and Inca spirituality included an elaborate cult to the dead known as *mallquis*, which generically included real and fictitious ancestral heroes that were often depicted as the founders of lineages, or extended households and communities known as *ayllus*. They were also often hailed as conquerors. Indeed, death was not the end of someone's interaction with the living; rather, life and death in the Andes was a complex issue that comprised a series of stages embodying the transition between life and death. So much so that in death there was the possibility of a person becoming a good, locally based *camaquen* ancestor, or a bad, wandering shadow *upani* spirit that drifted aimlessly, preying on people. It was this *camaquen* ancestor that became in turn revered and oracular, in essence a minor *huaca*.

If death and ancestor worship were a constant theme throughout Andean religion, then death was also part of the transitional and transformational process or renewal and rebirth intimately tied to the Andean concept of the 'origin place', or the *pacarina*. A *pacarina* was both the end destination of the dead and a community's place of origin. *Pacarinas* had a physical presence, which doubled up as places of worship centred around veneration of ancestors and the origin point of communities or lineages. It was *mallquis* and *huacas*, in their role as ancestors, that were intimately connected with these community birthplaces. Linking the various *pacarinas* in the Andean landscape was the fundamental element of water. Imaginary subterranean streams and rivers served to return the dead spirit to the *pacarinas* underground source and back again into the world. This served as a ritual of solidarity with the central or primary ancestor and a reaffirmation of community identity. In essence, then, death was the process by which humans became mummies, and in certain cases acquired 'aliveness' or *camac*: the first step in the process to becoming a bona fide ancestor hero, or *mallqui*. (Strangely analogous in some ways to how individuals become saints in the Christian, especially the Catholic Church.)

One final level of deity existed: that of the prime creator-god or gods. These changed across the Andes; for instance, the people of the Huamachuco region worshipped Ataguju and Catequil. Catequil himself also had an alter-ego known as Piguerao, and then there was Catequil's wife, Mama Catequil. In fact, the division of Catequil into so many aspects presages many common themes in Andean religion, and indeed society. This is the idea of internal separation into unequal reciprocal divisions. In this case Catequil had a homologous counterpart in Piguerao, but some deities were represented by two, three or even more aspects; Pariacaca, another central Andean deity, had five facets to his identity: Pariacaca, Churapa, Puncho, Pariacarco and Sullca Illapa, identified in the pertinent literature as his brothers. With many of these creator-gods there were subordinate kin-related shrines; for instance, Catequil had brother-shrines in Ecuador, while Pariacaca had the same in Northern Peru.

In the case of the Inca, these creator and ancestor deities were represented by Viracocha, as the creator-god, and Inti – the Sun – as the primary ancestor of the Inca royal lineage. Inti-Illapa, the Thunder God, was Inti's brother aspect, as was Punchao the morning Sun, and Mama Quilla the Moon was Inti's wife. All four male aspects came together as part of a four-part cosmological organization and were worshipped jointly in the Coricancha, the Inca Sun temple in Cuzco. Nevertheless, Viracocha had a less formalized, more distant form of worship somewhat removed from the exigencies of daily cult and affairs, these more mundane concerns being attended to by ancestors (*mallquis*) and other *huacas*. In the case of the four male aspects of Viracocha, Punchao seems to have been represented physically as a golden statue and therefore subject to more immediate adoration. This physical image of Punchao included a chalice which contained a dough made from dead *sapa* Incas hearts. The image was saved from the Spaniards capture of Cuzco in 1533 and taken into the Inca jungle redoubt of Vilcabamba, where it was venerated until that kingdom's demise in 1572.

The latent animism in Andean religion meant that, as with Greek and Roman gods, the relationship between deities and the world tended to imitate life. The organization of the Andean supernatural reflected many common social and cultural themes that were part of society. This was demonstrated by the often-tortured relationships between Andean deities, their concubines, wives, brothers and sons, and how they lived, fought, died, resurrected themselves and procreated. As the anthropologist Stewart Guthrie elegantly posited, 'man makes god in his own image.'

An adjunct to the whole pantheon of deities were female entities. Female deities seem to have had a more amorphous quality within Andean mythology, although this may well have been a product of post-European conquest bias and the decline of female agency and power during the early Spanish colonization. Among the female deities it is important to emphasize two in particular, the Pachamama (Earth Mother) and the Mamacocha (Mother

Lake), although many others existed, including Mama Quilla (the Moon), K'uychi (the Rainbow), celestial constellations and the dark patches between them. Apart from Mama Quilla, none of these important female entities seems to have been venerated directly in purpose-built shrines, although it is possible that small oratories to them existed. Mama Quilla may have been venerated at Copacabana on the shores of Lake Titicaca and at the Coricancha, in a separate room as the Sun's sister-bride. This concept of the female being venerated through, or in, the same place as the male might have existed throughout much of Andean cosmology. Thus, it is likely that the Pachamama – sometimes referred to as the wife of Pachacamac, the powerful *huaca* of the central Andean coast – was venerated in her own right within the large religious pre-cinct that made up the site of Pachacamac. Female deities appear more often than not as mothers, wives, consorts and sisters to male deities, although this in no way invalidates their influence on earthly matters. Once again, as in the case of male deities, the power of female manifestations to supposedly determine actions and events was mirrored in human society by the role played by women in important historical events, such as the numerous suc-cession crises that wracked the empire. Furthermore, veneration of the Pachamama was practised throughout the Andes.

Historically, female deities have been given short shrift in the literature, possibly as a consequence of both male bias on the part of the original Spanish chroniclers and because they predominantly occupied the lesser half of Andean cosmological divisions. Another common theme of many of these female deities was that they were often depicted as being manifest in important economic plants: Mama Sara materialized in maize, Mama Acxo in potatoes and Mama Coca in coca. It is possible, then, that female deities were of a slightly different type, less prone to overt violence (such as male deities), perhaps more universal and nurturing, as epitomized through their manifestation in crops. As such, their economic prowess would have added to their geographical universality.

Along their path to empire the Incas claimed both the Pacific and Titicaca Lake as their maximal *pacarinas*, linking their ances-tors and the creator-god Viracocha-Inti to them. This policy, akin to myth appropriation, had the dual purpose of restating Inca pre-eminence among other cultural groups, as direct descendants of the two largest and most prestigious of *pacarinas*, while also subsuming all local *pacarinas* and, by association, all deities and *huacas* under the mantle of the Inca Sun cult. Likewise, the *ceque*, a system of radial lines linking shrines, *huacas* and landscapes to individual Inca lineages, kin-groups, water rights and irrigation systems was itself exported to the rest of empire. Around Cuzco there were 328 shrines arranged radially as part of the *ceque* system, the same number of days as the Inca yearly calender. Away from Cuzco, these imposed *ceques* probably took over pre-existing pilgrimage routes that linked people and the surrounding living landscape. For instance, the placement of an Inca Sun temple within the precincts of the powerful coastal oracle temple of Pachacamac also indicated the ascendency of the Inca Sun cult and Pachacamac-Vichma's relative subordination to Viracocha-Inti. Similarly, it is possible that analogous *ceque*-like systems might have existed prior to the Inca ones in areas subsequently conquered by them.

But how different was Inca religious expression to that of the other Andean cultures? The founding myths of Pariacaca and Pachacamac catalogue the defeat of other peoples and their deities, akin to that of Viracocha together with Pachacutec Inca Yupanqui versus the Chanca and their idols. Similarly, there is evidence to suggest that many of the Inca ceremonies, for instance the *capacocha*, were not innovations, having existed previously among the cultures of north-central highlands. Therefore, the indication seems to be that the Inca were not so much innovators as collators of pre-existing *huacas*, rites and rituals brought under their control and the cosmological suzerainty of the Incan Viracocha-Inti deity. The change came in how they managed to integrate all these various ancestors, gods and deities into their pantheon. Nevertheless, Huayna Cápac's (AD 1493–1525) purge of extraneous ancestors and deities demonstrated that sometimes there could just be too many gods.

Other than major oracles such as Viracocha, Apurímac and Pachacamac, who had formalized temples and lands, and a hierarchically arranged organization of priests and attendants, it is likely that for lower-ranked local *huaca* there was a less formalized number of retainers or built-up temples. For instance, evidence shows that among the communities of Cajatambo and Recuay, in the north-central highlands, the rank of priest was chosen from among the constituent communities. Similarly, with the land given over to the *huaca* there seems to have been a more formalized division of it among the greater deities. These deities then officially had landholdings which were worked over by special retainers or communities, for the purposes of feeding the major *huacas* and their priestly attendants. That said, official literature on the Spanish campaign against idolatry in the Andes does contain numerous examples of local *huacas* with some access to attendant priests, retainers, fields and animals.

This parcelling of land for deities saw its maximum expression under the Incas with the division of land to important *huacas*, as well as to the different royal Inca *panacas*, or households. Considering that the Incas embodied deities in their own right, this is hardly a surprising development. At the local level, the difficulty that Spanish colonial authorities later had in disentangling community lands from *huaca* lands reflects on the much less clear-cut distinctions between these two types of land status (three if you include those lands assigned to the Inca). Most of the land and goods given over to the *huacas* were probably selected in an informal manner: as and when local ritual practice necessitated them, rather than specifically allocated as part of an Inca state agenda, or as a specified donation to the major *huacas*. A strict division between lay and religious property did not exist in the Andean world, especially given the divine status accorded to the Inca.

In essence, then, the root of Inca and Andean religion was that of an intensely ancestor-focused animism projected through oracular divination. In turn, this religion took in the totality of the landscape and environment as the stage, props and cue to a veritable dramatis personae of manifestations, happenings, spirits, ancestors and deities with which people related, combined and interacted. In this sense, Inca religion was not particularly different to its contemporaries. In fact, evidence suggests that

Inca religion, like the state, was probably in flux during the early sixteenth century. Given the relatively short duration of the Inca Empire at its height, it is likely that imperial institutions had yet to fully crystallize and cohere into a more durable and rigid form.

This can be seen in the problems that Huascar, the twelfth Inca (AD 1525–32), had in curtailing the power of the *panacas* of the eleven dead Incas that existed as *mallqui* by the time of his reign. Similar to the rest of Andean society, and the institution of split inheritance, when an Inca died his heir assumed the throne while the dead Inca's household (*panaca*) retained his property and lands while carrying duties of attendance to his now deceased, yet venerated person. Indeed, given Andean belief in ancestor worship and the life-in-death ethos, a former Inca was not dead and inactive; rather, he became a revered ancestor (*mallqui*), able to dispense judgement and order his lands and people through intermediaries. Some of these *panacas*, such as that of the ninth Inca, Pachacuti (AD 1438–71), owned vast amounts of property, were extremely powerful and had a propensity to oppose the dictates of the living, ruling *sapa* Inca. In opposing the *panacas*, Huascar was going against an older segmentary or heterarchical type of leadership that effectively curtailed the emergent imperial state and religious centralization.

While Inca religion emerged from similarly held beliefs within the broader tradition of Andean cosmology, it was also changing during the fifteenth century as a consequence of the experience of empire. This transformation was probably an effect of the exposures to new ideas that occurred during the Inca expansion, from such well-organized cults, including those of Pachacamac-Vichma and of the Chimor kingdom, along the central and northern coast respectively. This manifested itself in the attempt by the Inca state to create a pan-Andean cult exalting the *sapa* Inca (unique Inca) and the concomitant pantheon centred on the different aspects of the Viracocha deity – the Sun (Inti), Thunder (Inti-Illapa) and the morning Sun (Punchao). These also served to legitimize the Inca state in the newly conquered territories. It is intriguing to speculate how Inca religion might have developed had the Spanish never arrived, and had the empire reached a more mature stage with an all-embracing religious and political ethos to boot.

Unknown artist, *Pachacuti, Tenth Inca*, mid-18th century, oil on canvas.

The fragility of Inca state religion can be gauged by the ease with which local groups abandoned the central Sun cult of the Inca once the Spanish arrived. The reason for this is probably not that it was an alien concept, as has been claimed; many of the essential components of the Viracocha-Inti cult were present in other great Andean creator-god cults, such as that of Pachacamac-Vichma and Ataguju-Catequil, of the central coast and highlands respectively. Rather, the problem resides in that the Incas just did not have enough time to consolidate their Sun cult at the apex of a cosmological hierarchy that included all these numerous local and regional cults. Indeed, the Andes at this time enjoyed a plethora of local shrines and concomitant *huacas* that were only loosely

Red-ochre painted *huanca* of Pumpumyac, Pamparomas, Ancash, Peru.

tied to the Inca central religion. In the end, like the social, cultural and economic ties that welded the empire together, their foundations proved to be too shallow to survive the coming European onslaught.

In summary, while it lasted, Inca administration, administrators and the wider population were held together by a binding, though nascent, central ideological ethos. On the back of a pan-Andean animistic tradition, with a strong ancestor-worship cult, the Incas enshrined the divinity of their leader within a state religion that venerated the Sun (Inti), his wife, the Moon (Mama Quilla) and their creator-god Viracocha. Rather than suppress the beliefs of conquered people, the Inca subsumed local gods, holy sites or objects (*huacas*) and sacred standing stones (*huancas*) into their own ever-growing cosmological pantheon. These were all physically linked by pilgrimage paths (*ceques*) that ultimately radiated from the Coricancha (the Sun temple in Cuzco) to encompass the whole empire. Specific feast-days tied local festivals to their central equivalents in Cuzco. One such case is the *Yapaquiz*, or sowing of the corn, festival, which took place in August and commenced with the Inca symbolically breaking the sod in Cuzco. Local priests would then imitate this Inca action throughout the land, initiating the sowing of one of the most important crops in the Andes and the Inca Empire.

Such religious organization bound the empire together under the Villac Umu, or High Priest of the Empire, answerable only to the *sapa* Inca himself. Another religious sub-class were the *acllas*, a group of specially chosen women recruited from communities around the empire that served the Inca and his nobles as second wives, or concubines, among other ritual functions. From their ranks, the most physically perfect were sometimes selected for the ritual sacrifice of the *capacocha*. The practice of these special human sacrifices (usually of children or teenagers) at special sites such as mountaintops or even alongside lakes helped to link communities (who often offered these sacrifices) to the empire, binding them together around common rites and rituals that helped reaffirm the state in a local context.

In the end, crisis overtook this stressed system, first with the attempted reforms of the twelfth Inca, Huascar, and subsequently in the civil war between him and his brother Atahualpa, ending with the coming of the Spanish conquistadors and the disruption brought in its wake.

FOUR

Technology and Architecture

> . . . they were adepts in the arts of grading, of causeway-building, or terrace-making, and of tunnelling. What they lacked in mechanical appliances was amply compensated for by their ability to bring unlimited numbers of human hands to any task that they might undertake.
>
> PHILIP AINSWORTH MEANS, *Ancient Civilizations of the Andes* (1931)

The word 'technology' – from the Greek *techne*, meaning 'skills of science' – covers a wide range of themes and topics. With the Incas, and for the Andes in general, we can assess a number of technologies that, while existing in some cases prior to them, were perfected by them during the Late Horizon Period (AD 1450–1832). These we divide into three major types of technology: communications (roads and writing), economic (hydraulic and weaving) and constructive (architecture and town planning). All three broad technological fields intertwined in the formation of this unique Andean empire. A pristine empire, in which outside (essentially non-Andean) influences were non-existent or notably negligible.

In the 1960s the pioneering theoretical archaeologist Lewis R. Binford (1931–2011), following evolutionary anthropologist Leslie A. White (1900–1975), stated that given the social and physical exigencies of past human existence, culture served as the extra-somatic – that is, external to the body – means of adaptation by humans to the environment. In a similar vein, we can view all humans across the world as sharing a similar physical and mental hardware, in which culture, innovation and technology serve as the learnt, active software that guides the form in which people and society develops.

In the case of the Andes, millennia of almost complete isolation created an utterly unique series of societies culminating in the Incas. Societies with mores, knowledge and technology that the Spaniards often found inexplicable. For instance, Pedro Sánchez de la Hoz (1514–1547), a conquistador and Francisco Pizarro's personal secretary during the Spanish conquest of the Andes, marvelled at the Inca stone, wood and braided rope suspension bridges that spanned the vertiginous highland valleys. However, like many of his compatriots, he also feared them – especially the fact that they seemed to magically float in the air. Modern suspension bridges were only built by engineers in the nineteenth century, even though their use in the Andean highlands pre-dates this Western 'invention' by hundreds of years.

In the sense of communication technology, probably the single most impressive Inca monument was its road network known as the Capac Ñan covering some 40,000 kilometres (nearly 25,000 mi.) of road linking more than 2,000 settlements, administrative centres, way-stations or inns (*tampu*), storage facilities (*collcas*) and runner stations (*chasquiwasi*). Built across the austere highlands, verdant valleys and the oft mist-shrouded coast, the Capac Ñan knitted the empire together, allowing local authorities, as well as the Inca state, to keep tabs on the goings-on in the area under its control, moving armies, people and resources across the whole region. The pioneering Capac Ñan researcher John Hyslop (1945–1993) compiled the first large-scale survey of the road network in the 1980s, sometimes walking, riding, driving or even motorcycling along the length and breadth of it. His research served as the essential cornerstone of a recent multi-national application towards a successful UNESCO bid in 2014 that included Colombia, Ecuador, Peru, Bolivia, Chile and Argentina, which nominated the Inca highway as a World Heritage Site, similar in status to such other remarkable Andean archaeological sites such as Chan Chan, the capital of the northern Peruvian kingdom of Chimor, and Machu Picchu, a royal Inca lowland retreat of the ninth *sapa* Inca, Pachacutec Inca Yupanqui.

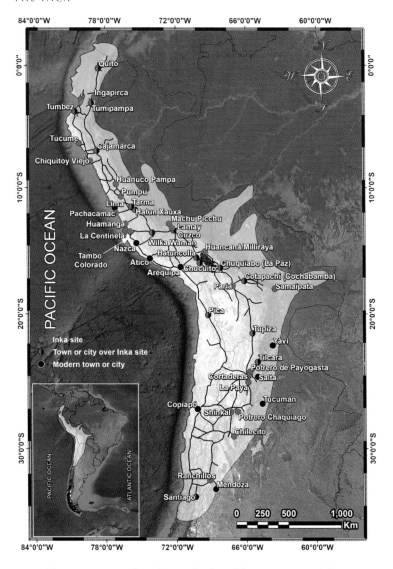

Map of the Inca Empire and road network, adapted from Terence N. D'Altroy, 'Funding the Inca Empire' (2014), and Martti Pärsinnen, *Tawantinsuyu: El Estado Inca y Su Organización Política* (2003).

While individual segments of the road system might seem modest, at its full extent it is an impressive feat of construction: a construction undertaken solely by human labour and, at most, stone or bronze tools. In particular, the major routes – especially

Collcas or storerooms at Ollantaytambo, Urubamba, Peru.

those leading to the north – were often over-engineered, with wide, well-proportioned and clearly demarcated tracks, zig-zagging stairways, and all the paraphernalia of a well-apportioned road, such as drains, culverts, buttressing walls and causeways. Structural architects turned Inca experts Graziano Gasparini and Luise Margolies have described this as an 'architecture of power', whereby the Inca sought to shock and awe the local populace with the functionality, aesthetics and scale of this endeavour. Equally, scholars have labelled monumental constructions such as this Inca network 'wasteful spending', in that it was over-engineered for its basic functional needs. However, it served as a testimony to the power of the Inca in being able to harness massive amounts of labour towards the construction and maintenance of this techno-logical marvel. Whenever and wherever you saw the Capac Ñan you knew you were in the physical presence of the Inca Empire. It is an enduring testament to its builders that, five hundred years later, huge tracts of this highway still exist.

Inca road, Santiago de Chocorvos, Huancavelica, Peru.

Essentially the main roads radiated from the capital Cuzco in four directions, to cover the four sectors of the Inca Empire, or Tahuantinsuyu, veritably the land of the four quarters. On top of this basic all-encompassing structure were myriad roads, routes and paths linking the provincial capitals of the empire, such as Shinkal, Pumpu, Tambo Colorado and Hatun Jauja, to each other through a complex web of ancillary structures (*tampu* and *chasquiwasi*), administrative centres and minor settlements. Among these provincial sites were a special type of settlements that doubled-up as 'new Cuzcos', such as Huánuco Pampa, Quito, Tumipampa, Hatunqolla, Charkas and Inkawasi. According to Incaologist Terry D'Altroy, these sites conceptually and cosmo-logically sought to replicate the Inca capital in the provinces, acting as centres of ceremony and ritual and aiming to reinforce the imperial ideal among the locals. This replication extended to these centres having their own local *ceque* system of imagined lines radiating from centres linking Inca concepts of kinship and cosmology through the employment of local shrines and pre-set pilgrimage routes.

In constructing this huge network, the Capac Ñan built on earlier paths, roads and routes – especially those of the previous Wari Empire (AD 600–1000) – expanding, rationalizing and helping to maintain them through the use of local corvée labour, known as the *mit'a*. Of all the constructions along the Capac Ñan it is the suspension bridges that have stuck in the mind of chroniclers, travellers and academics. At the height of the empire more than two hundred of these structures existed; anchored onto rock or specially constructed stone pillars, these rope bridges spanned Andean ravines and gorges. The most famous of these, the Apurimac Bridge, was described – and crossed – by the nineteenth-century explorer and archaeologist Ephraim George Squier in 1865; a scant twenty years later it had fallen into disuse. In its heyday it would have measured 45 metres (150 ft) across, and would have sagged downwards to stand just 35 metres (115 ft) above the tumultuous Apurimac River.

Nowadays only a couple of Inca bridges exist on the Apurimac River but near to the village of Quehue in Cuzco. Spanning the

Q'eswachaka rope bridge near Quehue, Canas, Peru.

river, which at this point becomes a 36-metre (118 ft) gorge, the bridge is rebuilt by the villagers every year in June from braided grass as part of an annual festival. In this sense, the yearly reconstruction provides an enticing vestigial insight into indigenous rituals, respect and the rhythm of work surrounding ancient Andean bridge-building. Able to withstand considerable weight, even while swaying dramatically, it is estimated that some of the larger bridges could have supported, at any one time, weight in excess of 90 tonnes. Indeed, the history of the conquest of Peru describes numerous bridge crossings, infamously including that of Sebastián de Belalcázar's bloodthirsty expedition of horse-mounted troops cantering over these splendid constructions to ransack Quito in 1534.

Impressive as the Capac Ñan was, it was the humble Inca runner, or *chasqui*, who best held the network together and connected the empire. It was they who conveyed messages and small parcels across the kingdom, working in relays of 6 to 9 kilometres (3–6 mi.) between the different stations or *chasquiwasi* (literally, 'runner-houses') and inns, or *tampu*. Transported in this manner, goods and messages could travel up to 250 kilometres (155 mi.) a day, such that a message from Quito to Cuzco (1,700 kilometres, or 1,055 mi.) took about a week. This was fast, especially considering the journey was made entirely on foot. According to the Spanish Chronicler Bernabé Cobo (1582–1657), the Inca received fresh fish from the Pacific Ocean by *chasqui*, the distance of roughly 350 kilometres (220 mi.) being covered in the space of less than two days. Highly athletic, trained and well-adapted to the low oxygen conditions of the high Andes, as well as the sweltering heat of the coast, the *chasquis* carried a *pututo* – a trumpet made from the shell of the Eastern Pacific Giant Conch (*Lobatus galeatus*) which grows on the coasts of Ecuador and Peru. The *chasqui* would blow his horn when approaching the next runner station (*chasquiwasi*), thereby alerting the next runner of his arrival.

While fresh fish and seafood on the plate of the *sapa* Inca, his wife and their attendants would have been highly desirable, the main duty of the *chasqui* was to convey information throughout the empire. This they did by transporting *quipu*, the knotted

CORE OV·MAIOR·I MEVOR
HATVNCHASQVICHVRV
MVLLO·CHASQVI·CVRACA

Depiction of a *chasqui* messenger from Poma de Ayala, *Nueva corónica y buen gobierno* (1615).

string device that the Inca used for record-keeping. No expansive political entity can exist without the means of keeping records, and the Incas were no exception. Yet the Inca did not develop an actual written language; instead, rather uniquely, they produced *quipu*: elegant, coloured strings or cords with knots that conveyed census, tribute and storage records, as well as serving to record more complex information such as narrative accounts, including genealogical data, property deeds and wealth. In transporting information, a *chasqui* would memorize a short oral message and carry a specially encoded *quipu*, elaborating on the message, which in turn a *quipucamayoc* or *quipu*-reading specialist would decipher. As with the earliest Middle-Eastern Sumero-Akkadian cuneiform, these *quipus* provided the necessary administrative sinews of the empire.

Quipu were composed of a thicker primary cord, made from a string of cotton or camelid fibre, from which pendant cords, with knots, radiated, and sometimes the pendant cords themselves had further strings (subsidiary cords) branching out. Archaeology now suggests that the *quipu* was not an Inca invention; rather, its roots lie with the Middle Horizon (AD 600–1000) Wari Empire, centred in the Ayacucho highlands. Theories that *quipu* might date all the way back to the Andean Late Preceramic Period (3000–1200 BC), however, remain fanciful. As previously mentioned, the Wari were also great road builders and it is enticing to ponder whether, like

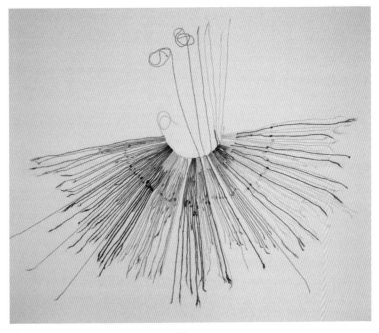

Quipu textile, *c.* 1400–1532, cotton and fibre.

the Inca, they too had a runner network similar to that of the *chasqui*. The fact that the Wari had a type of *quipu* also opens up the possibility of a greater degree of continuity in the dissemination of communication technology from the Middle Horizon across the first few centuries of social fragmentation and internecine warfare associated to the Late Intermediate Period (AD 1000–1450), through to the rise of the Inca.

As for the *quipu*, the colour of the strings, the position of the knots and the type of knot all conferred important information. Unfortunately, attempts to fully decipher the *quipu* have as yet been unsuccessful, given that for all the efforts of some early Spanish and indigenous chroniclers, such as Blas Valera (1545–1597), Inca Garcilaso de la Vega and Antonio de la Calancha (1584–1654), to relay how the *quipucamayocs* (the Inca cord-readers) encoded data and messages, they failed to faithfully record the myriad intricacies of the *quipu* coding system. What we do know is that two-thirds of the *quipu* use a decimal numbering code, which tallies with the Inca decimal-based administrative system, which it was probably counting as part of the information (especially census data of all kinds) entrusted within the *quipu*. The remaining third could well be a more narrative-based system of conveying the different types of data and information alluded to above, including genealogy, founding myths, history and legends.

Additionally, while the early Spanish administration used the information presented by *quipucamayocs* for settling taxes and property rights, the use of *quipu* declined sharply owing to the wariness of the Spanish towards a communication system that was controlled and understood exclusively by indigenous elites. Furthermore, the Catholic Church became increasingly concerned about the potential for heretical belief encoded and propagated by these strings. This led to wholesale burning of *quipu* and the active discouragement of further *quipucamayocs*. Exactly the same occurred in Central America with the beautiful Mesoamerican codices. Many of these were burnt as part of organized pogroms of eradication such that only four Mayan (as well as six other very fragmentary ones recovered from archaeological excavations) and about five hundred Aztec codices remain in existence. Similarly, only about 1,045 *quipu* are still preserved, of which the Harvard University Khipu Database Project has recorded in great detail more than 630.

Indeed, the vanguard of modern-day *quipu* research, including Carrie Brezine, Jon Clindaniel, Sabine Hyland, Viviana Moscovich, Frank Salomon and Gary Urton, among many others, suggest that a breakthrough is near. A recent study based on similarities between total numbers registered in a colonial census and a tax record carried out on the San Pedro de Corongo Indians from the Santa Valley, north-central Peru, in 1670, and knots on a *quipu* known as the *Radicati* or *Santa Valley Khipu* found nearby, implies that they may be counting one and the same thing. Even though this may be our first veritable 'Rosetta' *quipu*, we should qualify that while the information in both might be similar or the same, we are still a long way from deciphering the nuances and intricacies of the *quipu*. Suffice to say that an important first step has been taken, yet much more work still needs to be done if we are to get to the stage where we can truly 'read' Inca history.

Intrinsic to the *quipu* was the art of weaving and Andean civilization was a world pinnacle of cloth and textile making for its time. Facilitated by camelid fibres and pima cotton (*Gossypium barbadense*) from the coast, the indigenous populations of the Andes were skilled weavers who produced some of the finest quality cloth and textiles ever. It is possible that already by the Initial Period they had developed a variety of looms such as the backstrap, vertical and horizontal looms. Scholars have interpreted the textile production and its ostentatious use as the real measure by which wealth was calculated in Andean society. Similarly, a poor man was one who had no kin with which to exchange cloth.

Under the Inca, cloth was divided into two separate categories according to quality, *cumbi* being the higher and *ahuasca* the lower type. The first was woven especially for the Inca, his nobles and officials by female specialists known as *cumbicamayocs* or by the Inca's own chosen women, the *acllas* or *acllacuna*. *Ahuasca* cloth was much more of a household activity undertaken by commoners providing garments for themselves and as part of their tribute to local lords and the Inca state. *Cumbi* cloth and textiles in general

Cumbi high-quality Inca tunic, or *uncu*, with *tocapu* square patterning, 1400–1532.

were an integral element in the largesse that the Inca and his designated administrators dispensed to provincial lords as a means of ensuring their continued loyalty. So important were textiles to the Incas and their contemporaries that they were often used as a sacrifice to their gods and *huacas*. Cloth and textiles were also an essential element in the wrapping of their honoured deceased kith and kin, and integral to the creation of mummy bundles or venerated *mallquis* (sacred ancestors).

If roads and textiles united the Inca Empire, then it was human harnessing of the environment that provided the wherewithal for

Depiction of a mummy bundle from Poma de Ayala, *Nueva corónica y buen gobierno* (1615).

life in the Andes. In this respect, the key to civilization in South America was mastery over water. This mastery embraced the total transformation of landscape, rendering what was marginal and barren productive. It is no coincidence that the god of thunder in its many Andean guises – Illapa, Thununpa, Libiac, Pariacaca, Catequil – was one of the highest, if not the most important, deities within the Andean pantheon. For the Inca, Illapa formed part of a quartet together with Inti (the Sun), Viracocha (the Inca creator-god) and Punchao (the morning Sun).Indeed, water and the need to harness it was (and still is) a major concern for Andean indigenous communities, both on the sun-sodden coast – where, without irrigation, production would have been limited to the land along the riverbanks – and the vertiginous valleys of the cordilleras, where ample rains had to contend with severe slope run-off and strong atmospheric transvaporization (in the highlands, the extreme altitude heightens the degree of atmospheric vaporization of water).

Hydraulic technology was key to tackling these problems. Given the geographical divide of the Andes, this water-bearing technology can be roughly divided into coastal and highland types. Although there were some similarities in the technology used in both areas, for instance irrigation canals, there were substantial differences that derived from the divergent needs that local people had, as well as in the landscape, the peculiarities of water discharge and its overall availability. The coastal desert strip is mainly characterized by water flow, rather than water storage, as seen in features such as irrigation canals, filtration galleries and diversion embankments, which feed into a system dependent on floodwater and irrigation farming, while the highlands, with its vertical gradients, narrow valleys and highland alpine *pampas*, favour technologies that emphasize water storage. Also, coastal water technology is primarily targeted towards agricultural production, whereas the highlands display a more varied retinue of technological features that have so far eluded simple categorization into solely agricultural production. Indeed, in many cases highland water technology – even today – can serve the interests and needs of both farmers and herders.

Of Andean water-bearing technologies perhaps the most ubiquitous are irrigation canals: their function is simply to move water from where it is abundant to where it is needed. This, though, belies the potential complexity of irrigation networks, especially in hyper-arid places such as the South American Pacific Coast and

Irrigation canal, Cajabamba Alta, Ancash, Peru.

the high-altitude deserts that bestride the modern intersection between Argentina, Bolivia and Chile. Indeed, canal networks in the Central Andes are extensive, complex and ancient. Therefore, irrigation canals have a long history within the Andean region, especially along the dry coastal strip between the mountains and the sea. Claims have been made for the appearance of irrigation canals by around 3400 BC and perhaps as far back as 4700 BC in the Zaña Valley along the north coast. In fact, the whole of the coast presents a series of small to large canals criss-crossing the valleys, and sometimes even between valleys. In this sense, the coastal Moche (AD 200–600) and the Chimú or Kingdom of Chimor (AD 1100–1470) were known for their well-founded skills in hydraulic management and extensive canal building. This included the monumental Chicama-Moche Canal, built by the Chimor around AD 1200. Ostensibly built to counteract a lack of water in the Moche Valley, this 70-kilometre-long (44 mi.) canal ultimately failed after tectonic uplift, possibly due to earthquakes, rendered it unusable. Indeed, the archaeological evidence points to this remarkable engineering feature having never been fully operational, with only small sections working. In the end, all that effort for next to nothing.

While the scale of irrigation canal use in the highlands was lower, they were no less ambitious in their canal building. For instance, the (possibly Inca) Huiru-Catac Canal in the northern Ancash highlands runs for approximately 24 kilometres (15 mi.), bringing water from high-altitude lakes down towards highland terraces and eventually to the coast. Beyond the merely functional, irrigation canals held, and still hold, an important role within the social fabric of Andean communities, especially in the highlands, such that annual canal cleanings known as the *Yarqa Aspiy*, or 'water feast', are a community-wide event with a pedigree that reaches back into deep prehistory. During the Inca period, canal cleaning was part of the agricultural work undertaken during the month of *haylli*, which fell roughly in our month of August.

But perhaps the single hydraulic technology most associated with the Andes and the Inca are terraces. Cultivation terraces, or *andenes* (one of the possible origins of the word 'Andes'), are a water-based technology established around the creation of a series of level 'steps' on the otherwise sloped gradients of hills, ridges and mountains. In the New World, terracing has a long tradition across North, Central and South America. In South America their distribution is mainly concentrated along the central Andean area, the dry Pacific Coast, upwards into the semi-arid western Andes, and through to the cloud forest-clad flanks of the eastern cordillera towards the Amazon and the east-facing dry terraces of northwest Argentina. Until recently the earliest terracing in the Central Andes had been dated to around 500 BC, but now further research has pushed this date backwards to the Preceramic Period of circa 2480–2320 BC for the Colca Canyon in south-central Peru. Whatever their antiquity, the use of terracing was already well established by the Middle Horizon (AD 600–1000) under the Wari Empire. Nevertheless, it is widely recognized that terracing reached its apogee under the Inca Empire during the period known as the Late Horizon (AD 1450–1532).

Bench terraces, Miraflores, Upper Ica Drainage, Huancavelica, Peru.

While terrace construction led to some loss of land along the slope, it did bring with it four big advantages: it provided a stable platform for a bed of deep soil, which in turn helped cultivation; it controlled erosion and served as a buffer against the frequent landslides; it created a sustainable micro-climate; and it regulated soil humidity. Most terraces were constructed of fieldstone, with an inner layer of permeable gravel or rock. There are different varieties of terraces among them: check dams, cross-channel terraces, sloping field terraces, bench terraces and broad field bench terraces. Of these, the cultivation terraces typically associated with the Andes and the Inca were bench terraces, or *andenes*, but also known variously as *patasi*, *bancales* and *takhanes*. The most typical of these terraces were built of retaining walls made from closely fitted stones, usually to a height of between 1 and 5 metres (3–16 ft). Characteristically, they tended to be built along valley sides, presenting a panorama of visually stunning stepped vertical rows. These types of terraces were once ubiquitous across much of the Central Andes, and they still exist and provide subsistence in many valleys across the region, such as the Apurimac, Colca, Urubamba valleys, and along the Santiago and Tambo rivers in the Upper Ica Drainage.

Other hydraulic technologies existed, including pond-fields – *qochas*, or *qochawiñas* – which were small, shallow fields linked by canals, known on the coast as sunken gardens (*hoyas*, *wachaques* or *mahamaes*). There were also *amunas*, which stored rainwater and replenished underground aquifers; inundated ridge-and-furrow raised fields known as *camellones* or *waru-waru*, which ameliorated the harsh natural conditions of the plain around Lake Titicaca known as the *Altiplano* (literally 'high-plain'), artificial *bofedales* (known as *vegas* in Argentina and Chile), what we would describe as high-altitude peat moorlands, which served to geologically store water and provide rich pasture, as well as dams and reservoirs feeding water to terraces, fields and the aforementioned *bofedales*. The ubiquity of pre-Hispanic water dams has only recently been recognized, with these features reported across the Central Andes through to northwestern Argentina.

While the Inca cannot take credit for any of these innovations, they did greatly expand the range and scope of them from their Middle Horizon predecessors, opening up new lands to agriculture such that production rose across the empire. This grand harnessing of water led to a veritable series of managed landscapes across the

Yanacocha Inca dam, Pamparomas, Ancash, Peru.

Andes. Nevertheless, this management could sometimes go awry, hastening collapse through the ill-adjustment of some of these technologies to certain areas of the Andes. Indeed, the indigenous populations of the Andes were not immune to over-exploitation through farming, fishing or herding of their natural resources. Nor should they be viewed as hapless innocents in a veritable Garden of Eden; such a New Age interpretation of indigenous Andean culture risks reviving the age-old caricature of the 'noble savage', with all its precocious racism and denial of indigenous agency. That said, on the main, these technologies adjusted themselves exceptionally well to the exigencies of this land, a situation which took a decisive turn for the worse under Spanish colonial and Creole republican rule, such that many of these ancestral technologies were subsequently only partially maintained or not maintained at all, leading invariably to degradation, erosion and abandonment of vast tracts of the Andes – a singular European colonial legacy that indigenous people are still grappling with.

With the Incas, the construction and maintenance of hydraulic technology and bridge-building went hand in hand with incredible engineering skill – an expertise that they transposed on to their public architecture. Like their roads, Inca architecture was conspicuous in its detail, including rectangular shapes, trapezoidal entrances, windows and niches, gabled roofs, battered or sloping walls, and well-cut and bonded stones in both ashlar and polygonal patterning. An extreme version of the latter would be the polygonal walling of certain buildings in Cuzco, especially the former palace of Inca Roca, the sixth Inca, now the Museum of Religious Art. Indeed, nowhere was Inca architecture better showcased than in the imperial capital, with its upper and lower districts, royal palaces and plethora of temples. At its height, Cuzco must have been a sight to behold. This high-end Inca architecture, with its close-fitting, mortar-less polygonal and ashlar stonework, was both distinctive and, in many cases, earthquake-proof, such that the stones grated against each other under seismic activity before settling into their original positions. A similar anti-seismic building technique was used on stone dams throughout the Central Andes.

Ashlar stonework and trapezoidal niche, San Juan Bautista Church, Huaytará, Huancavelica, Peru.

Polygonal ashlar wall at Cuzco.

Square ashlar cancha enclosures at Kusicancha, Cuzco.

Given the ease of production, ashlar was always more popular than polygonal construction when it came to building across the empire. Throughout the empire this distinctive architecture was set into town plans that emphasized orthogonal (built along right angles) and radial (radiating from the centre) designs. Nowhere was this more evident than in the ostentatious construction of important Inca administrative centres such as Huánuco Pampa, Pumpu and Viracochapampa in the Central Andes. These centres almost always included a series of distinctive Inca buildings, such as *callancas* (administrative structures), *ushnu* (ceremonial platforms set within a central plaza), *canchas* (rectangular buildings usually located around the main plazas) and *collcas* (storage facilities), sometimes including less-common buildings such as the *acllahuasi*, which was reserved for the Inca's chosen women.

Likewise, the radial and orthogonal nature of these settlement sites may have also tapped into Inca notions of the sacred, manifested in the *ceques*. *Ceques* were imagined or idealized lines in the landscape around Cuzco that linked various *huacas* along the existing four-part division of the empire together with that all-important place in the Inca imaginary: the Coricancha, or Temple of the Sun. The sixteenth-century Spanish chronicler Juan Polo de Ondegardo (1500–1575) confirmed that more than a hundred sacred places and their attendant *huacas* or idols within the empire were organized along *ceque* lines. The radial nature of sites such as Huánuco Pampa and Xaquixaguana suggest this. As in the capital, so in the provinces with these places functioning as proxy Cuzcos. It is likely, then, that all these numerous sacred sites and *huacas* were then interlinked among themselves, serving to create almost an empire-embracing mesh of sacred places and nodes that reflected back on to the centrality of the imperial capital, Cuzco, and the divinity of the *sapa* Inca as the supreme interlocutor between the temporal and spiritual worlds of the Andes.

Finally, building to a design, Inca architecture or features thereof were exported to the far reaches of the empire, such that their distinctive style can still be seen from Ecuador (Ingapirca) to Argentina (Shinkal), served, as always, by the magnificent Inca road system. In turn this aimed at exporting the physical ideal of the Inca Empire in much the same way as the British did during the nineteenth century, transposing their Victorian Gothic revival architecture throughout their empire and beyond, for instance the Chhatrapati Shivaji Terminus (built in 1888 in Mumbai, formally Bombay) directly references St Pancras Station (built between 1862 and 1868) in London. Indeed, this architectural power ploy is a long-standing tradition for wannabe hegemonic empires ranging from the classical Roman forts to medieval Umayyad mosques, and onwards to the turn of the twentieth century and Austro-Hungarian green and yellow trains. All were enduring symbols of empire, expansion and embracive influence until their inevitable collapse, serving as reminders of what was, and then was no more. The Inca were no different.

FIVE
FEEDING AN EMPIRE

Ecologically, the area of the Andean republics seems at first
sight one of the least favourable environments for man . . .

JOHN V. MURRA, *La organización económica
del estado Inca* (1978)

Millennia of virtual isolation meant that pre-Hispanic
South Americans did things differently: we have already
described the *quipu*, their way of conveying language
through knotted strings; here we turn to the economy. Unique for
ancient civilizations, the Incas and their predecessors developed
an economic system almost without markets or commercial mer-
cantile interaction. Aside from the possible use of copper ingots
by Chincha traders, a coastal balsa-raft-using ethnic group from
the south-central Peruvian coast, in exchange for the coveted and
ritually valuable red-and-white lacquered Pacific thorny oyster
(*Spondylus princeps*) from Ecuador – literally considered the food
of the gods – or the exchange of T-shaped copper axes by specialist
traders, known as *mindaeles*, in central Ecuador and by the North
Peruvian Sicán culture, nothing similar to coinage existed across
the whole of South America prior to the coming of the Spanish.

This meant that goods were exchanged down the line by communities or persons from origin to destination through complex
systems of barter. These involved: llama caravanning; the transfer
of wares; reciprocity arrangements, such as the exchange known
as the *ayni*; gift-giving during unequal labour relationships, called
minka; or, under the Inca, via state-sanctioned labour obligations
or corvée systems known as the *mit'a*. Central for people's access to
varied resources, however, was direct control of different ecological zones using a system of discontinuous community territoriality
known as the 'vertical archipelago' model originally described by

Pacific thorny oyster (*Spondylus princips*).

John V. Murra, anthropologist and luminary ethnohistorian of Inca political economy in the 1960s.

These various systems were incorporated within the Inca Empire in its often-successful attempts to feed and maintain an empire of millions. Indeed, it is likely that the population of the Inca Empire peaked shortly before 1527 at around 12 million inhabitants, just prior to the first European epidemics against which indigenous peoples had no immunity. These epidemics began with a smallpox outbreak (AD 1524–8), closely followed by measles (AD 1531–3), then typhus and possibly pneumonic plague (AD 1546), and subsequently many, many more, including influenza and mumps. All of these wreaked havoc on the indigenous population. For instance, the smallpox epidemic in the 1520s – the first of more to come – severely impacted the Andes, even killing the ruling *sapa* Inca, Huayna Cápac, and his designated heir, plunging the land into internecine civil war soon after. The horror of imported disease and death was a constant during the first hundred years of European contact.

Nevertheless, before this populational catastrophe occurred, the Andes had been made bountiful by its people; a land capable of maintaining its expanding indigenous population due to enabling technologies (terraces, irrigation and so on) and abundant sources of food. It was also a land where two-thirds of its population lived in areas more than 3,000 metres above sea level; this is important when one considers that South America's truly expansive empires were always highland manifestations – Chavín, Wari, Tiahuanaco and the Inca – as opposed to the smaller, more circumscribed coastal polities such as Nazca, Moche, Sicán and the kingdom of Chimor. Western South America only became centred on the coastal regions with the coming of the seafaring Spanish, initiating a shift from the vast mountains to the freshwater-parched coast: a social and economic shift that has resulted in a steady and exorable populational shift from highlands to coast, with all the pressure on limited resources – especially water – that entails. Nowadays, especially since the 1970s, vast areas of the highlands have been abandoned, with villages and livelihoods disappearing across the Andean range.

Four main food-producing activities dominated Andean South America: fishing, farming, herding and hunting. Indeed, the economic narrative of the Andes has essentially been the contrast between highland and coastal economies. On the coast, fishing and shellfish collection provided the initial wherewithal for civilization's rise, while the highlands were instrumental in providing the load-bearing and protein-rich animal resources found in camelids. Indeed, we cannot begin to understand highland society and economies without the determinant role played by camelids in it. Without hyperbole, the cornerstones of expansive highland empires such as Tiahuanaco, Wari and the Inca (as well as possibly the earlier Chavín) were the llama and alpaca.

Turning first to the coast, fishing along the length of the Pacific Coast benefitted from one of the richest fisheries known in the world. While a wide variety of fish was consumed, the key coastal species exploited was Peruvian anchoveta (*Engraulis ringens*). Protein rich and abundant, the lowly Peruvian anchoveta may have been a prime instigator behind the move to sedentism by coastal populations during the Initial Period (3000–1200 BC). In turn this led to the agricultural cultivation of squash (for floats) and cotton (for nets), setting in motion early plant domestication. Likewise, inland freshwater fish such as *ipsi* and *carachi*, types of pupfish (*orestias*), were eaten by the local people that fished from highland lakes and rivers.

In the case of farming, the Central Andes was the location of what the eminent botanist and agronomist Jack Harlan (1917–1998) termed 'centers of diversity', in his seminal 1971 *Science* journal article entitled 'Agricultural Origins', meaning an area where autochthonous animals and plants were initially domesticated, before spreading in their cultivated form to other regions. Indeed, in the case of camelids, it represents one of the earliest instances of animal domestication in the Americas, having occurred around 5,500 years ago. Concerning plants, the area of the Central Andes stretching from the coast to the tropical lowland forest domesticated various varieties of beans, hot and sweet peppers, peanuts, squash and several fruits, such as guava, cherimoya, tomatoes, ground cherry or physalis. It is possible that certain types of starchy maize for use in *mote*, or hominy, and very early popcorn were also domesticated independently in the Andes, after the introduction of the original maize (*Zea mays*) from Mexico.

Another important Andean domesticate was coca leaf (*Erythroxylaceae*), which was used extensively as a sacred plant in pre-Hispanic and modern rituals. At present, as in the past, it is also generally consumed for its effects as a mild stimulant, in the same manner as the British drink tea and the indigenous Guaraní and Tupí (and nowadays Argentines, Uruguayans and southern Brazilians) drank yerba mate (*Ilex paraguariensis*). Drunk in a tea, coca leaf can also counteract the effects of altitude hypoxia, although it tends to be much more effective when chewed with a suitable alkaline such as ash (usually banana or sweet potato), bicarbonate of soda, baking powder or ground seashell. Coca

Rocoto aji hot peppers on sale at the Cuzco market, Peru, 2007.

leaf can also act as an anaesthetic and is incidentally a key component of modern cocaine and the original nineteenth-century Coca-Cola.

Yet possibly the greatest contribution to world plant domesticates, and a mainstay of the Andean diet, is the humble potato. With over 1,000 edible varieties, the potato was cultivated across the whole of the Andes from the coast to the lush eastern cloud forests. Hardy and versatile, it is nowadays the fourth most important world crop after maize, wheat and rice, according to the Food and Agricultural Organization of the United Nations. The indigenous population of the Andes also succeeded in dehydrating potatoes, making what is known as *chuño*, literally meaning frozen or wrinkled potato. This they achieved after a five-day process undertaken during the Austral winter at altitudes of above 3,800 metres (more than 2 mi.), where night temperatures regularly drop to −5°C.

Different varieties of potato on sale at the Cuzco market, Peru, 2007.

Chuño, or freeze-dried, dehydrated potatoes, on sale at the Cuzco market, 2007.

The process involves laying out the potatoes on the ground, where they are subsequently stepped on to squeeze out the juices, before allowing them to freeze and dehydrate overnight, repeating the process again the next day until the desired end product is achieved: that of a lightweight, desiccated, pebble-like shape. In this state they can keep for an exceedingly long time, providing an essential and vital stock of victuals.

The potato was first introduced to Europe at the end of the sixteenth century, and it had become the staple crop of large swathes of that continent and North America (where incidentally it was introduced from Europe) by the early nineteenth century. Such was European dependency on the potato that the spread of potato blight (*Phytophthora infestans*) in the mid-nineteenth century caused major famines and distress – especially in Ireland, where the potato famine of 1845 was in large part the reason for the current Irish diaspora throughout the world. In the Andes the potato, with maize and beans, formed part of that all-important carbohydrate triad central to Andean subsistence. Maize was also used extensively in the elaboration of *chicha*, maize beer, which was customarily enjoyed in pre-Hispanic and modern feasts, festivals and rituals. Maize (and potato) could also be stored for future use, either through drying or as *tocosh*. In making *tocosh*, potato and maize is placed in a bag or leaf-lined pit near flowing water. The potato or maize is then allowed to rot and ferment, after which it is removed from the pit and cooked either as soup or a jelly-like dessert known as *mazamorra*. A natural source of penicillin, it is also used in curing numerous ailments and is considered a delicacy in the Andean highlands.

Aside from the abundant fish of the coast, the greatest source of protein in the Andes was to be had from animals. South America had more domesticated animals than the Mesoamerican region, which only had dogs, ducks and turkey, but the diversity of domesticated animals was still limited in comparison with the Old World. In South America domesticated animal species also included dogs (*Canis familiaris*), typically the Peruvian hairless dog or *viringo*, and the Muscovy Duck (*Cairina moschata*). Both were eaten in the pre-Hispanic Andes. Dogs were brought over

Viringo or Peruvian hairless dog.

the then landlocked Bering Strait by the Western Hemisphere's erstwhile hunter-gatherer colonizers around 15,500 years ago. Additionally, the small but fecund guinea pig (*Cavia porcellus*) was, and still is, a reliable source of food and a traditional culinary delight of highland kitchens.

Nevertheless, the two greatest contributions to Andean meat protein were the llama (*Lama glama*) and alpaca (*Vicugna pacos*), the only two large domesticated ungulates of the Andes, and indeed the pre-Hispanic Americas. Given their differing physiology, they were bred for different purposes. The alpaca was reared primarily for their fine fibre, producing between 3 to 8 kilograms (6–18 lb) of fibre depending on breed and pasture. In the pre-Hispanic period alpaca fibre was used to fashion fine clothes and textiles. The llama is much larger and heavier than the alpaca, and before the arrival of the Spanish was South America's only beast of burden, able to carry 30–60 kilograms (66–132 lb) over distances of between 15 and 25 kilometres (9–15 mi.). Aside from fibre and transportation, camelids where also an important source of meat, fleece, leather, dung fuel and bones, the latter of which were useful

Llama, Antofagasta de la Sierra, Argentina.

Alpacas, Upper Ica Drainage, Huancavelica, Peru.

in the construction of tools. Their bezoars were also used in rituals and incantations.

The meat from camelids is naturally rich in protein and low in fat, with similar cholesterol levels to beef or mutton. As with potatoes and maize, it can be prepared for long-term preservation. This type of preservation is known as *charqui*, one of the few words to make it from Quechua into English as 'jerky'. *Charqui* was essentially salted and cured sun-dried meat, and it was a mainstay of highland-to-coast trade from at least the Early Horizon Period (1200–200 BC). As with *chuño*, it was lightweight, meaning that it was easily carried by llamas or porters. Camelids were ubiquitous to all the Andes and especially to the highlands, where they enabled the establishment of a herding way of life. Given the stacked vertical nature of the Andes, farming and herding tended to combine as agropastoralism in a particularly synergetic form much in the same way as goat and sheep herding and farming did in the European Alps, the Pyrenees and hilly Mediterranean islands such as Sardinia and Corsica.

The wealth derived from camelids, as well as their role in transportation, provided a lynchpin for many pre-Hispanic societies, such as the Late Intermediate Period (AD 1000–1450) Lupaca of the Titicaca Basin and Wanka of the Mantaro Valley. The white llama, or *napa*, was a royal symbol of the Inca. In fact, it is impossible to explain Inca expansion or their mastery of the Andes without their recourse to these animals.

Another important source of protein could be obtained through the hunting of wild camelids such as the vicuña (*Vicugna vicugna*) and the guanaco (*Lama guanicöe*), deer (*Cervidae*), small hare-like rodents such as the vizcacha (several genera of *Lagidium* and *Lagostomus*), as well as birds including the suri or ñandú (*Rhea*), among many others. The vicuña was also hunted for its fibre, which is finer than that from cashmere-producing goats. During the Inca period these animal captures were known as *chaccu*, and they were conducted yearly by the *sapa* Inca and his entourage. Rather than kill the beasts, they would herd them into temporary pens where they would be shorn before being released back into the wild. The fibre from these expeditions was used exclusively in clothes made for

Vicuña, Arequipa, Peru.

Guanaco at Torres del Paine National Park, on the border of Argentina and Chile.

the Inca and other designated elites within the empire. The reintro-duction of this type of capture-and-release method in the 1970s and up to the present day, albeit without the Inca or his retinue, is the single most important element in bringing back this animal from the verge of extinction, given that they had been indiscriminately poached and killed for their exquisite fibre.

Alongside food, the Andean region was also an important region for the exploitation of mineral resources, including tur-quoise, gold, silver, tin and copper. The Inca had reached a Bronze Age level of technology, having mastered the smelting of copper, tin, lead and arsenic to make both bronze and arsenical bronze. It was a pity that in encountering the Spanish they had to face up to a gunpowder-wielding, steel-using culture against which they initially had few weapons and limited success.

All these mineral resources were found in the Andean region. A key feature of the Andes is the stacked, vertical nature of the different ecological zones, such that it is possible to go from the coast to the Amazon by traversing less than 350 kilometres (220 mi.). Given the compressed nature of this environment and the almost patent lack of markets, John V. Murra suggests that, in the past, for a community to have access to all the resources necessary for subsistence it would have to control sections of land across various ecological tiers. This he termed the 'vertical archipelago': in essence meaning that a given community would physically colonize geographically distinct environmental 'islands', thereby gaining the resources within them for use by the wider commu-nity. This inter-community exchange would handle everything from fibre and leather, to fruit and feathers without the need for markets, relying on reciprocal exchange agreements that shared the various produce throughout the larger collective group.

The community group at the heart of this system was the Andean *ayllu*, a kin-based organization sharing a common ances-tor or origin. *Ayllus* often came in unequal pairs, emphasizing the duality at the heart of Andean society. Groups of paired *ayllus* could in turn become *llactas*, or hamlets, which in the context of the Andes basically meant a bounded territory of loosely linked people probably under the leadership of a hereditary or elected *curaca*, or chief. It is important to note that households in the pre-Hispanic Andean area tended to be dispersed throughout the environment, rather than bunched up in physical villages. Indeed, *llactas* were likely distributed across a whole swathe of the economically constituted vertical archipelago, under the guiding principles of *ayllu* endogamy and ecological exogamy (meaning that you married someone within your *ayllu*, but you went to live in a different ecological zone). A particular type of habitation site became ubiquitous during the period just before the rise of the Inca, the defensive hilltop settlement, or *pucara*. These proliferated in the latter part of the Late Intermediate Period, especially from AD 1250 to 1450, but it is likely that these were only fully inhabited in times of uncertainty and conflict.

There has been heated discussion as to the scale, range and temporal trajectory of the *ayllu* and its associated vertical archipelago, with some scholars disputing its existence along large tracts of the coast, arguing over how many ecological zones a community could control, and whether it was an early or late development in Andean prehistory. Suffice to say that it was in place by the Late Intermediate Period (AD 1000–1450) – just before the rise of the Inca Empire – throughout the highlands, with *ayllus* extending this vertical discontinuous pattern of control down the various watersheds both east and west of the Andean mountain range.

At its core, though, the *ayllu* was a decentralized system of governance, where community trumped individual leaders (*curacas*) and reciprocal obligations enshrined in the *ayni* ruled the roost. The *ayni* was the *ayllu* equivalent of 'you rub my back, and I'll rub yours': members of the community would pool labour and resources towards the common good. But this relationship between *ayllu* and leaders was not static. Against the violent backdrop of the Late Intermediate Period immediately preceding the Incas, internecine raids between rival *ayllus* and *llactas* precipitated the rise of fortified hilltop settlements, and with it the need for stronger leadership at the hands of appointed or god-ordained chiefs (*curacas*). This meant that by the time of the empire, the Inca increasingly faced groups organized around military leaders.

These *curacas* promoted a very different form of labour relationship: the *minka*. The *minka* was an unequal relationship between the leaders and the led, in which commoners' labour was exchanged for military and spiritual protection as well as largesse (cloth, *chicha* and feasts). The more a chief could potentially give, the more powerful they could become. These competing and contradictory forms of leadership – *ayllu* and *curaca* – and labour organization – *ayni* and *minka* – were at the centre of Andean society just before the expansion of the Inca Empire.

Indeed, the Inca can be seen very much in the light of having arisen from a similarly constituted highland society in the Vilcanota-Urubamba Valley around Cuzco. In many ways, imperial strategy mimicked the vertical archipelago on a much grander scale, exploiting the full gamut of Andean production across the four quarters of the empire and bringing with it a new type of labour organization: the *mit'a*. The *mit'a* was basically serf work. In a society where markets were scarce and money practically non-existent, human labour was the principal currency and main taxable commodity. So successful was this system that the Spanish appropriated it, especially for work in the mines, including the notorious ones of Potosi (silver) and Huancavelica (mercury).

Through the *mit'a*, the various *ayllus* and *llactas* of this Andean empire paid for their obligations to the state and also to the numerous *huacas* and their attendants, which in turn served as mitigation towards ensuring productive agricultural cycles. These obligations usually entailed up to two or three months of labour a year working on royal estates, or directly for the state on imperial infrastructure and economic production; it also included military service in the Inca levy armies. As with the *curaca*-led *minka*, the Inca also had reciprocal obligations to their subjects, including spiritual guidance, protection, as well as the maintenance and stocking of storerooms that could be used as a rainy-day fund for commoners, to restock passing armies and, critically, to guarantee the supply of produce for the numerous feasts and festivities of the Andean – and Inca – sacred calendar.

In this sense, during the Inca Empire, land and animals were divided into three unequal parts, those belonging to the *ayllu*, those of the state and those assigned to the various religious orders, especially the imperial cult of the Sun. Inca investment in farming and herding technology and infrastructure was in large part driven by the need to subdivide all available land and production into these three parts. Therefore, expansion of production under the Inca meant that less had to be taken from subject populations and local *ayllus*, given that the productive capacity of the different areas was augmented. Nevertheless, this was a policy that was bound to cause tension and resentment across the empire and would eventually provide a fertile breeding ground of allies willing to join the Spanish cause. Little did they know that the supposed cure was going to be much worse than the disease.

To run this vast organization of obligations, reciprocity and land management of the various local leaders, villages or *llactas* and *ayllus*, the Incas instigated new bureaucratic measures, including the introduction of a state-run administration with a class of people generically known as *yanaconas*. Once a *yanacona*, loyalty was to the Inca apparatus and no longer to their original *ayllu*. *Yanacona* were chosen for a life of service and taken out of their home communities forever, essentially becoming servants of the state on a plethora of different economic activities including domestic service, farming, fishing, herding, pottery, weaving and construction within Inca's state farms. As such they formed an alternative workforce for the Inca, outside of the *ayllu* system.

In very rare instances, a *yanacona* could even be elevated by the *sapa* Inca himself to the rank of lord; this happened to the lord of Collec in the Chillón Valley, near Lima. Here, following the death of the local leader in battle against the Inca, a *yanacona* was selected to the post. So useful were these *yanaconas* in their multiple roles that the Spanish kept many of these in place, to such a degree that the term 'yanacona' in some areas of the Andes became, during the colonial period, almost a synonym for traitor, given that they were seen to be in cahoots with the local priest and landlord in maintaining the Spanish landowning *encomienda* system.

The Inca also used colonists (*mitmas*) forcibly moved from their home communities to other areas throughout the empire, many varied specialists and artisans, and vast food storage facilities to serve local and military needs. The main Inca innovation towards managing the Andean economy was precisely this harnessing of specialists, known as *camayocs*, who were brought to bear on various aspects of provincial administration. Working closely with the Inca state and their elites, these *camayocs* undertook a huge number of activities ranging from smelting and herding, to torturing, weaving and soothsaying (in official temples), among others. Among the most important were the *quipucamayocs* (the Inca cord readers), the bureaucratic civil servants that essentially oversaw the empire. These administrative *camayocs* were responsible for the census and storehouses; they acted as secretaries, scribes, foremen and tax collectors, this last being an important function that they carried over into the Spanish colony. Given that the *sapa* Inca and his nobles were often absent, it was the *camayocs* that represented the human face of the empire at a local level. Skilled in the use of the *quipu*, they applied the empire's decimal numbering system to subdivide and tabulate the *mit'a* labour obligations of locals to the state.

The *mit'a* meant that several days' work every month were given over by able-bodied persons (usually men) for construction and maintenance of state infrastructure, including bridges, roads, buildings, fields, herds and so on. Ideally, the organization of this work was done on a decimal system whereby ten workers formed a *chunca*, ten groups of ten a *pachaca*, ten *pachacas* a *huaranga* (1,000), and ten *huarangas* a *hunu* (10,000). In reality, the decimal system had to accommodate itself to local idiosyncrasies, so while it worked well in the northern Chinchaysuyu quarter of the empire, it seems to have been less efficient in the southern Collasuyu quarter, possibly due to the scattered and dispersed nature of settlement in this sector. In turn, the four quarters of the empire comprised around eighty provinces, with each governor known as the *tocricoc*: an administrator plucked from the ranks of the nobility. Below each governor was a veritable army of bureaucratic officials, including *llaqtacamayocs* (town officials), *quipucamayocs* (cord-keepers) and *collcacamayocs* (granary masters), carefully running the empire. Aside from organizing the monthly *mit'a*, these *camayocs* were involved in administrating the empire's storage facilities.

Storage was critical to the empire. On the one hand it helped maintain the administration, including the armies as they camped or moved up and down the road network. Inca armies, mostly comprised of time-levied soldiery and a shock corps of elite Inca troops, could number up to 100,000 people or more, which gives an idea of the scale, complexity and efficiency of the Inca storage network. On the other hand, storage in the Inca Empire was primarily a local resource, rather than one which was transferred throughout the empire. Given the importance of labour as tribute, the lack of markets and the difficulties in moving wares – due to the absence of good draught animals in the Andes – it seems logical that storage fulfilled a different purpose to that of moving and exchanging goods and wares for a monied elite.

Rather, storage sat at the centre of a social, cultural and political complex that emphasized stockpiling for feasting and gift-giving by the Inca and his designated administrators at the regional and local level. This recalls the concept of the gift and the gift-economy as elaborated by the eminent sociologist and anthropologist Marcel Mauss (1872–1950), in which gift and feast-giving are essentially viewed as 'free' but actually entailed a three-part social exchange that reciprocally tied the receiver to the giver. This involved the giving of the gift, the acceptance of the gift and the return of the gift.

In the Inca economy, this meant the redistribution of largesse, the acceptance of these goods and the precepts of the Inca state by the *ayllus*, and finally the obligation by these same local groups to contribute in labour towards the state. This was an unequal relationship in which the Inca always held the upper hand in any exchange with other human cultural groups. Indeed, the Inca viewed this *mit'a* relationship very much as a type of *ayni*, where the *ayllus* gave their labour in exchange for food and *chicha* (maize-beer). In turn, the food and beer were produced by the *acllas* or *acllacuna*. The concept of gift-giving extended to alliance building, whereby provincial lords gave a selection of their most beautiful women to be the Inca's chosen women (the *acllacuna*);

this took the concept of Andean human capital as tribute to its logical extreme. These women served the Inca and the Sun cult, and were also pivotal in cementing alliances through bride-giving between the Inca and prospective allies.

These women, and especially chosen children, were the ultimate gift in the only relationship to which the *sapa* Inca might have felt subordinate: that of himself with the supernatural. This was the *capacocha* (royal obligation), the ritual sacrifice of people (and animals, especially camelids) to the numerous oracles and spiritual manifestations that so inhabited Andean cosmology and landscape. The *capacocha* sacrifices were conducted on mountaintops, sacred lakes, such as Lake Titicaca, and other spiritually imbued places throughout the empire. That said, mountaintop sacrifices seem to have been more common in the southern portion of the empire, while lakeside *capacochas* were more frequently practised in the north. As yet, we cannot explain the reasons behind this difference.

The best-preserved example of an Inca *capacocha* are the three frozen children of the Llullaillaco Mountain, located in modern-day Argentina. Aged around six, seven and fourteen, they seem to have been given a special diet for a year prior to their sacrifice to the gods. Buried with sumptuous grave goods, including effigy statuettes, decorated *spondylus* and shells as well as many other items, the Llullaillaco mummies were not deposited at the same moment in time; rather, they were spaced out, reflecting the need to periodically renew this sacred royal sacrifice between the Inca, or his representative, and the supernatural. It is likely that the dominant theme behind the *capacocha*, that being the concept of elite gift-giving to the gods, pre-dates the Inca. In this sense, there is evidence of sacrifices of children and animals by local groups at cosmologically imbued places such as lakes, while the spectacular sacrifice of over 140 children and 200 camelids at the Chimor site of Huanchaquito-Las Llamas on the northern coast (dated to circa AD 1450) demonstrates that sacrifices to metaphysical manifestations of weather phenomena – in this case most likely the erratically cyclical El Niño weather pattern – provided the context for conspicuous gift-giving to placate the gods.

As for stockpiling, the physical nature of storage meant the building and maintenance of a vast complex of storerooms across the empire. The main repositories for these storerooms were Cuzco itself and its major provincial centres, or 'other Cuzcos' such as Tambo Colorado, Pumpu, Huánuco Pampa, Hatun Xauxa and Shinkal. These places served as the nexus for feasts and gift-giving to the local populace and were also major staging posts for armies on the march. Further down the scale most smaller centres also had their own storage facilities. The typical storage unit, known as a *collca*, was a round or square modular structure of usually one or two rooms built from fieldstone. At the largest centres these were built in their hundreds. Huánuco Pampa, the prime administrative centre in the north-central Andes, had close to five hundred such structures without taking into consideration the numerous processing and administrative structures within the town itself. Other sites had many less *collcas*: for instance, the small administrative site of Intiaurán in the Upper Nepeña drainage only had about fifteen such storage facilities. These administrative centres and their *collcas* thus served as the cornerstone of a decentralized system of controlled production that radiated from the capital, Cuzco, to the various provinces.

While it is possible that *collca*-like storage structures had existed prior to the Incas, maybe even under the Wari Empire (AD 600–1000), the scale of storage by the Inca Empire was unparalleled in Andean history. That said, the level of storage also varied throughout the empire, with many more structures located in the northern Chinchaysuyu quarter, as opposed to the southern Collasuyu one. This has been interpreted to signify that Inca control and presence in the south was of a different magnitude to that in the north – in this sense, much more indirect and at arm's length. While this may well be true, it does fail to take into consideration a type of storage that was very prevalent in the south, possibly much more than in the north: what one could call storage-on-the-hoof (or on the pad, given the anatomy of South American camelids).

The vast pasturelands of the south, from Lake Titicaca through to northwestern Argentina, represented a region ideal for rearing camelids – especially llamas, the mobile, load-carrying backbone of the Andes. It is estimated that at the moment of European contact in AD 1532, there were in the region of 30 to 50 million camelids in the Andes. As mentioned previously, animals, like land, were divided into unequal thirds: commoner herds-of-the-weak (*huaccha llama*) versus the elite (Inca and religious order) herds-of-the-powerful (*capac llama*). The *sapa* Inca had many tens of thousands of animals belonging to him personally, as well as the wild vicuña, which could only be captured by himself and his designated people. For instance, the Temple of the Sun apparently had more than a million camelids assigned to it; these massive herds were known as the *intip llaman*, the llamas of the Sun. Other temples and *huacas* had their own animals, too. Indeed, the appropriation of camelids by the Inca and incoming religious cults when conquering a new area or province was a particular grievance of many local *ayllus*, once again undeniably serving to show the material and symbolic importance these animals held for Andean people.

The final major piece of imperial control strategies of production was that of the *mitmas*, also known as *mitmacuna* or colonists. *Mitmas* were communities including women, children and animals that were moved wholesale around the empire to satisfy the various administrative, economic, military or strategic interests of the empire. The scale of this movement was vast; chroniclers such as Bernabé Cobo (1582–1657) claimed that a full third of the empire's population was transferred from one place to another. In essence this meant somewhere in the region of 3 to 4 million people, a formidable number when one considers that all movement had to be done on foot. While it was claimed that the ninth ruling Inca, Pachacutec Inca Yupanqui (*c.* 1438–1473), commenced this *mitma* policy, it was really during the time of his grandson, Huayna Cápac (1493–1525), that it reached its apogee.

While in many cases the *mitma* movement would have meant solely the transfer of the population from their Late Intermediate Period (AD 1000–1450) fortified hilltops down to the valley below – such as happened with the resident Wanka populations in the central Andean Mantaro Valley – in other cases, it could signify the mass shift of large numbers of a community to the far-flung reaches of the empire, to serve on royal Inca estates such as Abancay (southern Peru) or Cochabamba (eastern Bolivia); or on the religious sanctuaries located around modern-day Copacabana (northern Bolivia), Lake Titicaca, including the Temple of the Sun and Moon on their homonymous islands; or, more usually, to places to produce or extract particular goods and wares for the empire, such as weaving, herding, mining or maize farming.

This fundamental economic rationale was accompanied by an equally important strategic one, such that populations transposed to a foreign region tended to be less recalcitrant and therefore more loyal to the state. Furthermore, given that locals normally resented the presence of these new colonists on their lands, it meant that in turn the *mitmas* were bound tightly to the Inca state. They were *ayllu* without local ties with all the negative connotations that brought with it under the Andean community concept of kin obligations and ties of reciprocity. Equally, *mitmas* expanded the productive capacity of the empire by bringing new areas into cultivation and use. Incidentally, it has been very hard to identify and separate *mitma* colonies from local groups archaeologically, leading some scholars to speculate that it might not have been as widespread a phenomenon as the Spanish chroniclers seem to have initially thought.

Even so, the whole policy was riddled with problems. The *mitmas* often retained rights in their original *ayllus* and regions, which meant that complete severance was almost never possible. Likewise, the intense nativism of Andean populations, a parochialism reinforced by the landscape and limitations on travel, meant that these wholesale movements were often bitterly resisted by the wannabe colonists. Such was their propensity to relapse and move back to their parent communities that fines were imposed on offenders by the Inca authorities. Indeed, with the coming of the Spanish and the collapse of the Inca Empire, many *mitmas* just packed up and returned to their communities.

Another type of – often forced – movement that occurred within the empire was that of the sons of local *curacas* and lords sent to Cuzco as hostages and students. There they were inculcated into the ideology of the empire before being sent back to their native regions to spread the ethos of *pax incaica* while serving as provincial administrators. Also held as hostages were effigies of local gods or *huacas*. These were housed around the temples of Cuzco and subordinated to the imperial gods, reinforcing physical subjugation of the people with a metaphysical one of their *huacas*.

By way of conclusion, we can see that the bounteous seas, stark deserts, glaciated mountain ranges, highland tundra expanses and jungles made the Andes a challenging, yet extremely rich and highly compressed, environmental landscape. The distance from the coast to the jungle at the height of Cuzco is only 400 kilometres (250 mi.), and in other areas even less than that. Likewise, in a north–south direction the empire stretched from the coastal fjords of Chile to the Argentine northwest, and northwards to the verdant tropics and sun-blushed coasts of Ecuador and Colombia. This vast empire was home to a rich biomass (fish, camelids, tubers, maize, beans, fruits, cotton and so on) and immense mineral wealth, including gold, silver, copper, obsidian and turquoise, which the Inca and their subject people exploited fully.

Long described as a paternalistic socialist economy by the likes of German Marxist theorist Heinrich Cunow (1862–1936) and French economic scientist Louis Baudin (1887–1964), the Inca were much more complex than that, welding indirect and direct methods of governance with control over local resources and people, together with overarching responsibility for the supernatural. The main commodity in the Andes was human labour, and this was organized by the Inca across three types of equal and unequal reciprocal or gift-giving arrangements: the *ayni*, *minka* and *mit'a*. These were supervised by a retinue of state servants known as *camayocs* selected from among the local populations, including the *mitma* colonists, which allowed for expanded production with new lands being brought under use. *Yanaconas* also fed into this state apparatus as an *ayllu*-less group, undertaking many menial and necessary tasks on Inca estates and farms. Young women were picked to serve as the *acllas*, the Inca's chosen women, acting as servants and concubines, in ritual sacrifices (*capacocha*) and as gifts to seal alliances and pacts with potential allies. Young high-status men from the provinces were brought to Cuzco to be instructed in the ways of the empire. In return, the state promised to provide feasts and gifts as well as up-keep of the roads and monuments, and protection.

By the time of the Incas, goods, fields and animals were divided into three lots: those of the Inca, the religious temples, or *huacas*, and the *ayllu* community. Work on the former two was done through recourse to the *mit'a*, the *mitmas* and by *yanaconas*. This was especially so on royal estates, which belonged personally to an Inca and subsequently to his household upon his death.

At the local level, communities organized their economy through recourse to a vertical archipelago of resource exploitation, in which they would hold rights to territories at different altitudinal levels or ecozones, thereby achieving a remarkable degree of self-sufficiency. Some of these vertical control systems – such as in the southern Peruvian Moquegua Valley – extended from the circum-Titicaca Lake and Altiplano area all the way down to the coast. More compact or compressed systems, linking a smaller number of stacked ecozones, existed throughout the Andean highlands, especially further north. The localized system of the vertical archipelago encouraged a self-reliance that the Inca later reinforced through provincial capitals and their localized storage (*collca*) networks. This provincial centralized system of storage also provided a safety net for moments of scarcity, as well as feeding the armies and administrators of the state.

In return for participating in this highly regulated economy, the *ayllus* could be guaranteed an acceptable standard of living and, crucially, a degree of safety. Harsh laws – including ones on house cleaning, theft, adultery, failure to render service and food to the *huacas* and so on – helped to keep the people in check and ensured a high level of order and personal hygiene in the Andes – much higher than that present in large areas of Europe at the time. Indeed, the Inca could be seen to have provided a primitive form of welfare state, where the concerns and tribulations of the communities were absorbed as much as possible by the state and resolved by its governors and administrators.

Yet the empire was no panacea, and resistance to the Inca – especially by the recently subjugated people of the northern frontiers of the empire, the Cañaris and Chachapoyas, but also throughout other parts of the empire – grew, especially after the death of Huayna Cápac and his designated heir in 1525. His successors, Huascar and Atahualpa, could not manage to hold the empire together, and as civil war ripped the Inca elite apart, the land was ripe for conquest. Into that emerging power vacuum entered the Spanish.

SIX

INCA POLITICAL POWER

> The first point is that there do in fact exist rulers and ruled, leaders and led. The whole of the science and art of politics is based on this primordial, irreducible (in certain general conditions) fact.
>
> ANTONIO GRAMSCI, *The Modern Prince and Other Writings* (1957)

All empires are by their very nature transient; sooner or later, they all collapse. Rome, the so-called Eternal City, was sacked by the Visigoths under Alaric in AD 410, and the Sun had called time on the British Empire by 1970. Between those two historical extremes, empires have come and gone – Spanish, Portuguese, Austria-Hungary and Ottoman, among many others. Some, like the Napoleonic First French Empire (1804–15) were a flash in the pan, while the Byzantine – or East Roman – Empire (AD 395–1453) lasted well over 1,000 years.

The Andes proved no exception to the rule. Before the coming of the Incas, the widespread highland phenomenon known as the Chavín Horizon (1200–200 BC) and the two Middle Horizon empires of Wari and Tiahuanaco (AD 600–1000) demonstrated both the extent and limits of potential South American imperial enterprises, confining them essentially to the highlands and the central western seaboard of South America. Similarly, the Inca, likely borrowing from Tiahuanaco and especially Wari statecraft, expanded exponentially throughout western South America with control extending to the southwestern border of modern-day Colombia, the eastern foothills of the Andes, the edge of the *yungas* area in northwestern Argentina and the narrow valleys of south-central Chile. The Inca created the biggest indigenous empire of the American continent. Incidentally, and underscoring the importance of camelids as a food and transport source to South America, the limits of the Inca Empire coincided rather neatly with the natural range of the llama.

Undoubtedly, the death knell of the Inca Empire was the coming of the Spanish, yet vested interests within the imperial state, especially between local forces and wider imperial politics, were providing increasing stress to the body politic, leading eventually to the Inca Civil War of 1529–32. Essentially, the powerful centrifugal force of the state and organization of Inca control were increasingly pitted against that of the local Cuzco *panacas*. The *panacas*, from the Quechua root word *pana*, meaning 'brother's sister or cousin', were segmentary, *ayllu*-like organization of hereditary royal houses built around the veneration of ancestral mummies, or rather life-in-death Inca kings. While containing many similarities to the *ayllu*, it was a term particular to the Inca.

Therefore, while it is true that the Inca, like most Andean people, observed parallel descent, that is, sons descended from fathers and daughters from mothers, the fact that the term *panaca* is rooted in a female suffix indicates that something else is at play here. To explain, the Inca also practised split inheritance, where a new *sapa* Inca ascended the throne with the title and little property, while the recently deceased Inca kept his household (*panaca*) and reign-accumulated wealth. In these circumstances, the latter's main attendants were his female relatives, the same female relatives that would subsequently provide the ruling Inca's main wives (known as *coyas*). As such, a number of scholars have loosely interpreted the *panaca* as a group of brothers and their sisters who have descended along matrilineal lines from a common male Inca ancestor. This was a group whose members practised exogamy: marriage outside the lineage group. Indeed, the marriage between a *sapa* Inca and high-ranking *panaca* women (usually the Inca's sisters, half-sisters or close cousins) ensured two things: first, the support of his wife's *panaca*, and second, support for the Inca's sons and erstwhile heirs through recourse to their mother's *panaca* lineage. In Andean – and Inca – society the role and agency of women was underestimated by Spanish chroniclers. Only recently are scholars deciphering the true power of women in this society.

Also, at the heart of the *panaca* was veneration of a dead Inca. Veneration of the dead had a long pedigree in the Andes, but with the Inca and the *panacas* it was taken to new extremes. For instance, by the time Huascar came to the throne in 1525 he had to contend with eleven *panacas* of sacred deceased kings, each with their own agency and political agenda. This agenda was inherently conservative, aimed at preserving the rights and prerogatives of their particular household. No wonder that Huascar attempted to restrict them in a bid for stronger centralized control and govern-ance. Needless to say, at this turn of events by Huascar, most of the *panacas* then allied with his half-brother, rival and eventual successor, Atahualpa (*r.* 1532–3). The rise and fall of the Incas have to be understood under these dual, and sometimes competing, lens of royal and *panaca* power, their respective roles in succession and governance, and what this meant for how the empire evolved towards its eventual nemesis.

Both the standard and long timelines for Inca history provide a relatively short chronology – between 95 and 150 years – for the rise of the empire. In all respects, then, this expansion had been at a vertiginous rate, and state and community institutions struggled to keep pace with its growth, which at its largest extent stretched over 4,000 kilometres (nearly 2,500 mi.) from northern Ecuador, down to northwestern Argentina and Chile. Given the pressures of managing such a vast empire, it comes as no surprise that the expansionist Incas of the fifteenth century, especially the last undisputed Inca, Huayna Cápac (*r.* 1493–1525), were attempt-ing to renew the institutions of the empire, escalating the use of colonists (*mitmas*), regulating the flow of labour tribute (*mit'a*), while seeking to professionalize the army.

These reforms went hand in hand with others to ameliorate the inherently unstable and complex system of Inca succession, by instituting first, possibly under Pachacutec Inca Yupanqui (*r.* 1438–71), the designation of a principal wife (or wives) – the *coya* – of the Inca from whose sons the next Inca would be selected. While this did not always succeed, with often the most able or ruthless making it to the tasselled throne (the Inca insignia of royalty was the *mascaipacha*, a tasselled fringe), it established at least some sort of basic order to their royal inheritance system. This was followed by a further, more drastic, reform under Topa Inca Yupanqui (*r.* 1471–93), which ruled that the Inca's *coya* had to be his full sister (although in the end this usually meant his half-sister, first cousin or female relatives of the same generation). Given the number of secondary wives and concubines, this was seen as a means towards controlling potential successors to the throne, and it was not unheard of for the Inca to have numerous full and half-brothers killed off upon ascending (something that Topa Inca Yupanqui and Huayna Cápac certainly did early in their reigns).

In so far as succession was concerned, the essential problem at the centre of Inca royalty could be said to be the lack of primogeniture within Inca power politics. Even in countries with primogeniture – such as feudal Europe in the ninth to fifteenth centuries – the eldest did not necessarily inherit the throne. But primogeniture established a set of rules that could, and would often, be followed. The lack of such a clear line of succession brought serious instability to the Inca inheritance system, in which the strong and ambitious could oust the weak and less able. It also brought in its wake periods of chaos that would wreak havoc on the nascent institutions of the empire. A look at the last four Incas before the Inca Civil War between Huascar and Atahualpa demonstrates the convoluted nature of Inca succession.

Starting with Pachacutec Inca Yupanqui, the paean to his glorious, god-divined triumph over the perennial early Inca bogey-men, the Chancas, was nothing more than a storytelling ruse to cover his usurpation of the throne from his father, Viracocha Inca (*r. c.* 1410–38), who he sent into exile, and the designated heir, his older brother Inca Urcon, who Pachacutec subsequently had killed. For good measure Pachacutec also wiped out Inca Urcon's whole household, a tactic that was to be reused by Atahualpa against Huascar. In turn, Pachacutec's son, Topa Inca Yupanqui, had at least one brother – Amaru Topa Inca – removed from the scene, enabling him to ascend the throne unopposed. Topa Inca Yupanqui's long stewardship of his father Pachacutec's later reign, his successful military campaigns and his royal pedigree seem to have ably positioned him to successfully jockey for the *mascaipacha*. However, ability was not necessarily always a prerequisite for survival. Pachacutec had other successful Inca military captains – including his own brother, Capac Yupanqui – executed. In Capac Yupanqui's case, execution came after his successful campaigns in the north-central Andes. You could be successful, but you had better not be *too* successful.

It was Capac Yupanqui's death that led to Topa Inca Yupanqui's ascendency and eventual elevation as Inca. Not that he fully enjoyed the fruits of his success. The ethnohistoric evidence suggests that Topa Inca Yupanqui struggled at the beginning of his reign to garner the support of the other Inca *panacas* in Cuzco: he was eventually assassinated, either through poisoning or by an arrow, while at his royal estate in Chincheros in the Sacred Valley, near the capital. Topa Inca Yupanqui's designated heir, conceived by his full sister, Mama Ocllo, was Titu Cusi Guallpa, later known as Huayna Cápac. (It was quite common for Inca heirs to change their name on gaining the *mascaipacha*.) Yet Huayna Cápac's path to the throne was also contested by another of his brothers, Capac Guari, son of a secondary wife of Pachacutec's, Chuqui Ocllo.

Huayna Cápac was still young when these events occurred, and his suit was pressed by two uncles, Gualpaya and Guaman Achachi. In turn Gualpaya, a military leader and possible co-ruler under Topa Inca Yupanqui, attempted to seize the throne for himself, before being dispatched in turn by Guaman Achachi. On finally attaining the throne, Huayna Cápac had two other brothers executed and erased the wannabe usurper, Capac Guari, and his household from most official histories.

Huayna Cápac followed all the necessary traditions, selecting his full sister Cusi Rimay as his *coya*. Unfortunately, Cusi Rimay died in labour giving birth to her only son, Ninan Cuyuchi. This single scion of the union between full brother and sister was proclaimed principal heir to his father, Huayna Cápac. Nevertheless, Ninan Cuyuchi never got his chance at the *mascaipacha*, dying days apart from his father from the same smallpox epidemic that swept through the Andes in 1525 while still a relative youth of between ten and twelve years of age. This set the scene for the final denouement of the Inca Empire and the visceral civil war waged by two other sons of Huayna Cápac – Huascar and Atahualpa.

This brief jaunt through the succession travails of the last three Incas before the civil war demonstrates how complex and dangerous inheritance of the empire could be, both for the winners and losers. These moments of crisis were made even more convoluted by the role played by the *panacas* – the royal households of dead Incas – and courtly intrigues of the various wives and concubines of the ruling Inca. In turn, many of these women belonged themselves to *panacas* and were therefore habitually engaged in furthering the interests of their own section, household and, in the case of wives or mothers from regions outside Cuzco, those of their geographical areas. This occurred when Paullu Inca (later Cristóbal Paullu Inca; 1518–1549) ascended the Inca throne in 1537; his mother, Añaz Colque, was from the Huaylas province and her son favoured that region.

Incidentally, neither Huascar's nor Atahualpa's mothers were *coyas* to Huayna Cápac, although Huascar did have his mother marry the mummy of Huayna Cápac in a bid to further legitimize his claim to rule. This example of necrogamy was only possible because the dead in the Andes retained a degree of agency and vitality in accordance with their status in life and observable oracular powers in death. As deceased-yet-living divine beings, the Inca royal dead wielded considerable power through their *panacas*.

As alluded to earlier, the *panacas* were the households created around the figure of a *sapa* Inca at the time of his death. The Inca practised split inheritance, whereby the heir to the throne inherited nothing except his authority, while the remaining wives, concubines, sons and daughters of the dead Inca formed a *panaca* that took care of his body and became part of the ritual *ceque* system around Cuzco. From within the ranks of the new household, a person or persons speaking for the dead Inca in his living-in-death oracular capacity were selected. These *panacas* held on to the lands and estates conquered or adjudicated to them during the life of the titular Inca and could hold considerable authority in the regular councils and deliberations with the ruling Inca. This was especially true of powerful *panacas*, such as that of Pachacutec Inca Yupanqui (Hatun *panaca*, although he was initially of the Iñaca *panaca*) and Topa Inca Yupanqui (Capac *panaca*). The prestige of these households was not centred on how old the *panaca* was, but rather how much it possessed, which is why later households, particularly those of Pachacutec, Topa Inca and Huayna Capac, with vast property gained through conquest were particularly influential.

Hurin Cuzco	
Manco Capac	Chima *panaca*
Sinchi Roca	Raura *panaca*
Lloque Yupanqui	Auayni *panaca*
Mayta Capac	Usca *panaca*
Capac Yupanqui	Apo Mayta *panaca*

Hanan Cuzco	
Inca Roca	Uicaquirao *panaca*
Yahuar Huacac	Aucaylli *panaca*
Viracocha Inca	Socso *panaca*
Pachacutec Inca Yupanqui	Hatun (formerly Iñaca) *panaca*
Topa Inca Yupanqui	Capac *panaca*
Huayna Cápac	Tumipampa *panaca*

Inca King list divided into upper (*hanan*) and lower (*hurin*) Cuzco and their *panaca*.

As previously mentioned, the *panacas*, in comparison to the *ayllus*, were matrilineal, and therefore a medium through which women could wield influence and power. Indeed, given that a ruling Inca only founded his household at the time of death, during life he maintained close ties with his mother's kin and *panaca*. Furthermore, in the Andes at this time women were not in as subservient a position as their counterparts in Europe, or as they would later be under Spanish rule. In a highly dualistic society (one divided into unequal, reciprocal halves), women invariably occupied the lower half, while men belonged to the upper one (lower and upper were known respectively as *hurin* and *hanan*, and were the classic dual division present throughout Andean society). Nevertheless, the relationship between men and women in Andean society, and especially among the ranks of the elite, was essentially complementary. Therefore, ruling Incas usually selected their *coyas* and secondary wives from the royal households to cement their power and alliances in Cuzco, as well as with the *panacas*. Women from influential households were much sought after. In turn, these women maintained ties with their original households and strove to further the *panaca*'s interests through their sons and the advantageous marriage of daughters. Women also owned land and resources in their own right, giving a solid foundation to their power.

No woman was more powerful than the *coya*, the principal wife of the *sapa* Inca (usually his full sister or in some cases his half-sister or first cousin). Half-sisters and first cousins were also ranked as full sisters under Inca kinship terminology. There could be more than one at any one time. The marriage and union of the Inca to the *coya* was seen as recreating the original sacred couple of the Andes, the so-called *yanantin*, the marriage between the Sun (father) and the Moon (mother). As mothers to the prospective heir, they wielded considerable influence, especially if their son attained the *mascaipacha* while still a youth, as seems to have happened with Huayna Cápac. In this respect Mama Ocllo's swift action following the death of her husband, Topa Inca Yupanqui, was instrumental in securing the throne for her son, Huayna Cápac. The power of women in these affairs of state is underlined by the fact that periodically the women from particular households were also selected for termination during the various succession crises. When Atahualpa defeated Huascar in 1532, he had him and all his family, including a large number of his mother's kin from the Capac *panaca*, executed. In fact, such was his rage and anger at this *panaca* that he had the mummy of Topa Inca Yupanqui – the titular head of the Capac *panaca*, and his paternal grandfather – burnt.

The deliberate destruction of one's direct ancestors was an extreme measure in a culture that so venerated the dead. Yet this radical action demonstrated two things: one, that the *panaca* was rooted in matrilineal concepts. Atahualpa belonged through his mother, Tocto Ocllo Cuca, to Hatun *panaca*, Pachacutec Inca Yupanqui's household. Therefore, Atahualpa only visited destruction on his patrilineal side. And two, that it was possible to effectively wipe out a royal household. Destruction of Topa Inca Yupanqui's mummy and household could easily have paved the way for the eventual eradication or relegation of this *panaca*, and shows how Inca history, based as it was on oral tradition, could be – and probably was – periodically rewritten. This might explain why there were extra-*panacas* that did not figure with a personage on the king list. These included in the *hanan* half of the king list, the Cusco and Iñaca *panacas* (to which Pachacutec Inca Yupanqui had originally belonged), while in the *hurin* half of the same list there were the Masca, Sauaseray and Yauri *panacas*.

In turn, the *panacas* were linked to ten non-royal *ayllus* (Chauin Cuzco, Arayraca, Guaycaytaqui, Tarpuntay, Sañoc, Sutic, Maras, Cuicusa, Masca, Quesco), which had places named after them in the Cuzco region. These ten *ayllus* all had ancestors with acquired, imagined or projected links to either the Inca origin myth (as in the case of the Maras) or to the original inhabitants of the Cuzco area, and as such they were of higher status than the provincial *ayllus* of the commoners. The relationship between the aristocratic *panacas* and non-royal *ayllus* demonstrates yet again the unequal, reciprocal duality at the heart of Inca, and Andean, social structure. This leads us to an equally thorny subject related to the convoluted Inca succession system: how was Inca rule organized?

Arcane arguments about how Inca rulership was effected have raged since the 1960s. It might seem an overly esoteric discussion, but it is important for understanding how the Inca projected themselves and their power throughout the empire. These scholarly discussions have oscillated between what we will call the orthodox view, that the Inca were a standard single-ruler monarchy, and the non-orthodox view, that the Inca king list reveals a diarchy (rule by two) or even triarchy (rule by three) at play. The problem is compounded by the fact that all scholars researching this base their arguments on the same early ethnohistoric accounts. Ethnohistoric accounts often written by Spanish chroniclers who themselves were trying to make sense of what they saw or what they had interpreted from indigenous witnesses. In essence all these sources are flawed, and the truth within them, as it is, can be reinterpreted in many different ways.

Nevertheless, with respect to Inca rulership and sifting through the different arguments and co-arguments for single monarchy versus different forms of co-rulership, it seems plausible that, given the inherent dualism of the Andean worldview, some form of co-rule might have existed within the empire, with a ruling *sapa* Inca and a weaker, attendant co-ruler. This would go a long way towards explaining the intriguingly close association between the ruling Inca and a number of fringe characters in Inca narrative history, such as Capac Yupanqui, Amaru Topa and Tarco Huaman, among others. Indeed, in the ultimate expression of duality, the person of the *sapa* Inca himself was divided into two, one part containing his physical human self and the other his brother icon, or *huauque*, which accompanied him in life and death and could even officiate for him at rituals, in battle ceremonies and public events. This is why the *sapa* Inca could quite literally be in two places at the same time.

We know that the Inca king list, like much of Andean society, was divided into two separate halves, belonging respectively to the lower (*hurin*) and upper (*hanan*) dynasties. Traditionally, this king list has been viewed as being sequential, in that two follows one, three follows two and so on. Yet a closer look at the matter of the king lists, starting with R. Tom Zuidema and his meticulous analysis of the sources, suggests that Manco Capac, the first *Sapa* Inca, was the common, possibly mythical, ancestor to both lineages, and that the subsequent *hanan* and *hurin* lists were coeval rather than sequential, with the *hurin* personage serving as a sort of ruling understudy to the current *sapa* Inca. This was further elaborated by the eminent French ethnohistorian Pierre Duviols, who developed a variation of the kingly list such as the one below:

1 Manco Capac

Hanan Rulers	*Hurin* Rulers
6 Inca Roca	2 Sinchi Roca

7 Yahuar Huacac	3 Lloque Yupanqui
8 Viracocha Inca	4 Mayta Capac
9 Pachacutec Inca Yupanqui	5 Capac Yupanqui
10 Topa Inca Yupanqui – Tarco Huaman (?)	
10 Topa Inca Yupanqui – son of Tarco Huaman (?)	
11 Huayna Cápac – Tambo Mayta, Don Juan (?)	
12 Huascar Inca – Tambo Mayta, Don Juan (?)	

Inca rulers divided into upper (*hanan*) and lower (*hurin*) dual king lists.

Immediately we can see that all twelve standard Incas are included in the list, alongside other individuals such as Tarco Huaman and Tambo Mayta. Intriguingly, Topa Inca Yupanqui seems to have had two co-rulers of the same lineage: Tarco Huaman and his (unnamed) son. This split between the *hanan* and *hurin* Cuzco household would also explain how Capac Yupanqui could be Inca in his own right, as well as brother and commander of Pachacutec Inca Yupanqui's forces in the north.

Indeed, considering the many anomalies that emerge within the written sources concerning the contemporaneity of many of these individuals with each other, duality and some sort of diarchy – including the actions of a *sapa* Inca's effigy double, or *huauque* – would seem the most logical explanation for this confusing plethora of names, peoples and overlapping roles. In this sense, perhaps the best example of a possible functioning diarchy is the joint conquests of Pachacutec Inca Yupanqui and his son, Topa Inca Yupanqui, during the former's later reign. With advancing age (he lived until his late fifties or early sixties), Pachacutec seems to have stayed in Cuzco more and more, delegating the expansion of the empire to his son and heir. Here might be a model for co-rulership, in which the *sapa* Inca and his second performed different, though complementary, functions within the Inca state. An earlier example would be that of Viracocha Inca (eighth ruler) and his son Inca Orcon, before Inca Urcon's precipitate death at the hands of his brother, Pachacutec Inca Yupanqui.

It seems that in most cases the second 'ruler' engaged in the running of Cuzco, or some other aspect of Inca statehood. For instance, another potential secondary Inca (with a different function) was the figure of Amaru Topa, another son of Pachacutec. Some sources relate that he was originally selected as the heir to the tasselled throne but that he was too gentle for the rigours of power – his main interests lying in water engineering and agriculture – so he was demoted, and his brother Topa Inca Yupanqui stepped up to take his place. Nevertheless, it is possible that Amaru Topa and other, eventually less worthy, individuals maintained a differential relationship with power at the apex of Inca society. In the case of Amaru Topa, this relationship involved being charged with oversight of infrastructure projects and economic well-being.

The relative anonymity of Tarco Huaman and his descendants as secondary rulers to Topa Inca Yupanqui, Huayna Cápac and possibly Huascar suggests that, as the Inca state developed, the power of the diarchy weakened, with authority vested increasingly into the figure of the *sapa* Inca and his *huauque*. Indeed, it could be that the ostensible duality among early Inca rulers became less so as the power of the state and more vertical forms of government became both more popular and desirable. Similarly, moves to curtail the power of the *panacas*, especially by Huascar, could be viewed in much the same light.

Finally, and rather dizzyingly, there are other king lists, advocating further divisions of power including a triarchy (rule of three), with Orcon, Amaru Topa and Paullu Inca making their appearance as secondary or tertiary rulers. The culmination of all of this endless replication were probably the pre-eminent Peruvian ethnohistorian María Rostworowski's views on the matter. She took the duality subdivision to its logical conclusion when considering the four-quartered Tahuantinsuyu and gunned for four ruling Incas, each with his own quarter, with that of the northern quarter (Chinchaysuyu) governing as a first-among-equals over the others (followed by the Antisuyu as its *hanan* female counterpart, and then Collasuyu as the *hurin* male division followed by the Cuntinsuyu *hurin* female division). In this constellation, the most important *sapa* Inca was also the direct ruler of the Chinchaysuyu. In a similar vein, certain scholars have further suggested that each Tahuantinsuyu quarter, or *suyu*, might have had its own *pacarina*, or 'mythical place of origin'.

What all this confusion about Incas, women, duality and royal households says to us, however, is that the Spanish did not quite grasp the intricacies of Inca rulership: how it was articulated between the highest echelons of society, and how the *sapa* Inca, in turn, negotiated his authority with the *coyas*, secondary wives, concubines and *panacas*. What is equally true is that the institutions of Inca government were in a state of flux at the beginning of the sixteenth century: a deep process of reorganization that the Spanish disrupted and selectively dismantled, keeping and perverting certain institutions, such as the people–state labour obligations known as *mit'a*.

Through this process of state creation, reformulation and consolidation, one figure that appears again and again is that of the Villac Umu, the high priest of the Coricancha, the Temple of the Sun in Cuzco and the religious centre of the empire. Possibly established under Pachacutec Inca Yupanqui, the position of the Villac Umu, second only to the divinely ordained *sapa* Inca, was the maximum religious authority in the empire, charged with protecting Punchao, the sacred image of the morning Sun. He was selected from among the *panacas* and was therefore a descendant of one of the royal Inca lineages. Irrespective of whether he originally came from *hanan* or *hurin* Cuzco, he became a member of the lower half upon being Villac Umu. In a partnership of the sacred in the Inca Empire, the *sapa* Inca retained ultimate divine authority in yet another unequal relationship with the Villac Umu, this time centred around spiritual power and authority. Yet the Villac Umu retained considerable authority, especially in endorsing a new *sapa* Inca through the placing of the *mascaipacha*. Although mostly serving in a religious capacity, they did also sometimes serve as army generals, especially under Atahualpa and Manco Inca, the latter being one of the neo-Inca rulers of the rump Vilcabamba kingdom (1537–72), established after defeat at the hands of the Spanish in the early 1530s.

Aside from the Villac Umu, the *sapa* Inca was served by Incas of royal blood: the members of the various *panacas*. As we have seen, this was a double-edged sword; these individuals' loyalty was primarily to their household, and the dead Inca sitting at the top of that particular power pyramid. Nevertheless, Incas of royal blood formed a large influential group within the society and politics of Cuzco, and included brothers, sisters and nephews and nieces down various iterations of kinship ties to the ruling Inca. Together they formed the *Incacuna* (the Inca people), their ranks furnishing administrators and governors in the provinces, generals for the armies, and soldiers for the royal bodyguard or elite corps – the nearest the Inca had to a standing army. As the Inca's blood kin, they formed the familial bulwark and royal court of the empire, although, as mentioned previously, this loyalty was constantly tested by the pull of their *panacas*.

Below them were the Inca-by-privilege. These were members of non-Inca groups from the Cuzco region. In part, they also made up the bulk of the *ayllus*, associated with the *panacas* mentioned above, and through intermarriage with members of these same royal households became secondary kin, or what the indigenous chronicler Felipe Guaman Poma de Ayala termed *huaccha* Incas (literally 'poor Incas') to the *sapa* Inca. In total, Inca-by-privilege came from the 26 different ethnic groups found within the Cuzco area such as the Mayu, Anta, Poques, Urcos and Chilque. This Inca-by-privilege social class filled the intermediate level ranks of administration and were mostly confined to running, both economically and ritually, the core lands around the Inca capital, Cuzco.

Alongside the Inca-by-privilege were another minor elite class, these were the lords-by-privilege. Lords-by-privilege were individuals elevated to positions of power personally by a given Inca, similar to the *yanacona* lords mentioned earlier. The position was normally non-hereditary and could be revoked at a moment's notice. Detached from the *ayllus*, these lords-by-privilege owed their position and power solely to the Inca, and as such their loyalty to the ruler was paramount. Examples of these individuals are found in early colonial sources, such as the case of Pedro Astaco, whose father, a servant of Topa Inca Yupanqui, was elevated to the lordship of a town near Cuzco. Almost a type of super *mitma*, an important function assigned to them was to govern recalcitrant or distant regions.

Below these various categories of Inca and privileged ranks came the native lords of the land. Conquered, or persuaded by the Inca to join them, these lords could be powerful personages in their own right. Evidence suggests that the Inca themselves – at least in the highlands, where power had tended to be both heter-archical and segmented – promoted the concept of single or dual leaders, or *curacas*, for the different provinces. The coast already had a long tradition of rulers or kingdoms such as Chimor, Ychma and Chincha, along the North, Central and South coast respec-tively, but the highlands had been notoriously Balkanized since the fall of the Tiahuanaco and Wari empires during the eleventh and twelfth centuries. Having a lord hold sway over a larger area of land made it easier for the Inca (and afterwards the Spanish) to govern. Some of these lords and their people, such as the lord of Chincha, were loyal subjects of the Inca. The lord of Chincha was given the distinct honour of being carried on a litter like the *sapa* Inca himself; he was eventually killed at the hands of the Spanish while still holding the royal litter during the capture of Atahualpa at the Battle of Cajamarca in 1532.

Other lords, especially those who had but recently been incor-porated within the empire, were much more circumscribed in their loyalty. It was they, as well as the followers of Huascar – the defeated party in the Inca Civil War – that first went over to the Spanish, with dramatic consequences. Securing loyalty was always a problem for the empire; in the fiercely independent Andes of the Late Intermediate and Inca Period, loyalty was first to one's *ayllu* or community, or, in the case of the *panacas*, to their dead liege lord and household. Therefore, given the highly personalized nature of Inca conquest and their policy of split inheritance, prac-tically every new *sapa* Inca had to go on numerous campaigns to subdue the manifold rebellions that tended to flare up upon the death of the previous *sapa* Inca. The chronicles are replete with stories of the various campaigns that new rulers had to engage in before being able to initiate wars of conquest, and this is probably why, when tabulating conquered lands, the deeds of certain Incas repeatedly show the same places being conquered and brought into the empire. For instance, Huayna Cápac spent the first years of his reign pacifying and expanding the south of the empire, as well as putting down major rebellions in the Titicaca area and along the north coast of Peru. Only then did he feel free enough to engage in conquering campaigns to the north, towards modern-day Ecuador and into the very southern border of Colombia, ultimately the furthest northern extent of the empire.

In conclusion, at the midpoint of the third decade of the sixteenth century, the Inca Empire was at its peak of expansion but dragging with it myriad problems stemming from rapid growth and insufficient reform of the sinews that held the state together. Local *ayllus,* regional lords and Cuzco itself, divided between the *panacas,* non-royal *ayllus* and Inca-by-privilege, all vied against the centralizing tendency of the *sapa* Inca and state institutions such as the lords-by-privilege, the *yanacona,* the *acllacuna* and the *mitma.* Every empire has a breaking point, and although predicting the point of collapse is often a futile exercise in hindsight, the auguries for the future of the Inca Empire must have been foreseeing storm clouds. They would have been right: within ten years the Inca had all but collapsed, and with them one of the most powerful, resplendent and unique empires the world had ever seen.

SEVEN
CRISIS, PANDEMIC AND COLLAPSE

The hand of the Conquerors, indeed, has fallen heavily
on these venerable monuments, and, in their blind and
superstitious search for hidden treasure, has caused
infinitely more ruin than time or the earthquake.

WILLIAM HICKLING PRESCOTT,
History of the Conquest of Peru (1847)

Sometime during 1525, as Huayna Cápac lay dying in Quito
with a high fever from the smallpox epidemic (possibly combined with measles and malaria) that swept the Inca armies
fighting in the north against Colombia-based tribes, he called for
the *mascaipacha*, the tasselled fringe and insignia of Inca rule to
be given to his son and heir, Ninan Cuyuchi, then between ten
and twelve years of age. Under Inca succession tradition, Ninan
Cuyuchi, the only son of his full sister and wife, was supposedly
next in line, even if he was only a callow youth. Little did Huayna
Cápac know that his young son would soon die or had already
died a few days before from the same disease that felled him and
ravaged the empire.

The death of Ninan Cuyuchi opened the field to a contested
succession, a common enough feature in Inca history. Without
a clear successor born of a *coya*, the crowded field of prospective heirs was as large as Huayna Cápac's numerous progeny. This
included at least two hundred – possibly as many as three hundred
– children, a rather substantial number of which would die in the
subsequent Inca Civil War. From among this vast field of brothers
and half-brothers, two powerful individuals with strong ties to
different *panacas* emerged to vie for the throne: Cusi Hualpa better

Unknown artist, *Huascar (Guascar), Thirteenth Inca*, mid-18th century, oil on canvas.

known to history as Huascar, of Topa Inca Yupanqui's impor-tant Capac *panaca*, and Atahualpa, son of Tocto Ocllo Cuca, of Pachacutec's influential Hatun *panaca*. In the end no fewer than five different sons of Huayna Cápac would ascend the throne, three of them under Spanish aegis.

Accounts concerning what exactly happened around the death of Huayna Cápac vary, although general consensus among these sources is that he first designated Ninan Cuyuchi as his heir but the soothsayer auguries came back with a negative (Ninan Cuyuchi was himself already dying or dead). Then the increas-ingly sick *sapa* Inca called on Huascar as his heir, but, likewise,

Unknown artist, *Atahualpa, Fourteenth Inca*, mid-18th century, oil on canvas.

the augurs reported in the negative. When the priests returned one last time, they found Huayna Cápac dead. Emissaries were then sent to Tumipampa, near modern-day Cuenca in Ecuador, to inform Ninan Cuyuchi and his potential co-ruler and half-brother, Atahualpa, about their ascension. Ninan Cuyuchi was dead, however, and the path to the throne lay wide open to any ambitious royal Inca parvenu.

Of the early sources, Inca Garcilaso de la Vega, the important Inca-Spanish *mestizo* chronicler of the early Spanish colony, alone states that Huayna Cápac actually called for split rule, with Huascar in the south and Atahualpa in the north. Garcilaso could have done this out of an attempt to whitewash history and render it much more in tune with European medieval standards of kingship and feudal division of land between siblings. Alternatively, and much more plausibly, Inca Garcilaso de la Vega did this to blacken the name of Atahualpa, given that Garcilaso de la Vega himself was of the maternal lineage of Huascar and therefore also a member of the Capac *panaca*. By portraying Huascar as accepting his father's division of the empire he makes out Atahualpa to be the greedy brother, unsatisfied with his paltry lot.

Indeed, the story as recounted by Inca Garcilaso de la Vega makes a monster out of Atahualpa. In Garcilaso de la Vega's retelling, Atahualpa was an illegitimate scion of the noble Huayna Cápac who brutally abused and usurped the goodwill and naivety of his legitimate half-brother, Huascar. In this, as in all his writings on Atahualpa and his maternal *panaca*, Pachacutec's Hatun *panaca*, Inca Garcilaso de la Vega had an axe to grind. Indeed, he further delegitimizes Atahualpa by alleging that his mother was not even from Cuzco, but rather a native princess from the Quito area in modern-day Ecuador. Had this been the case, Atahualpa's claim to the throne would have been tenuous indeed, only able to claim the royal tassel on his patrilineal and not on the all-important matrilineal *panaca*-based side.

Interestingly, in the circumstances surrounding Huayna Cápac's death agency and action passed once again to women, in this case Raura Ocllo, Huascar's mother, a member of Topa Inca Yupanqui's Capac *panaca*. Following Huayna Cápac's death, she swiftly left Quito and hurried south to Cuzco to warn her son about his father's untimely demise, while gathering support among the royal households towards the investiture of her son. Huascar had stayed behind in Cuzco while his father had been successfully campaigning in the north, perhaps even as a co-ruler. Concurrent with Raura Ocllo's precipitate actions, Huayna Cápac's funerary cortège left Quito for Cuzco, but importantly, without Atahualpa or the dead Inca's victorious and battle-tested northern generals: Chalcochima, Quizquiz, Rumiñavi and Ucumari. Huascar, singularly displeased at having supposedly 'left behind' his half-brother in the north, had the nobles leading the entourage apprehended near Limatambo, on the approach to Cuzco, and subsequently tortured and executed. This killing of emissaries would not go unpunished in the subsequent bitter civil war.

With his father's mummified remains firmly under his control, Huascar had his mother marry it, thus making her Huayna Cápac's legal *coya*, or royal wife, and further legitimizing Huascar's hold on the throne. Huascar also married his full sister, Choque Huypa, ignoring his mother's objections on this point. Yet the failure to have captured Atahualpa during the first months of his reign clearly rankled Huascar; accounts tell of his rage against his mother and sister for having left the north without him in tow. Huascar ordered Atahualpa to come south, but he remained ensconced in the north, sending obsequious gifts in exchange. These were not only patently rejected by Huascar, but he had the messengers killed, and, for good measure, made drums with their skins. To add insult to injury, Huascar sent Atahualpa presents of women's clothing, cosmetics and jewellery, possibly alluding to his manhood, or lack thereof. All in all, an emphatic message – if any were needed – that returning to Cuzco would mean Atahualpa's death. Atahualpa's constant prevarication at this stage of the proceedings can be interpreted as deft delaying tactics, while he marshalled his forces composed of his father's loyal northern troops and generals. These were tried and tested warriors with whom he had been campaigning for years. They also supported Atahualpa's claim to the *mascaipacha*, and the potential prerogatives and privileges that would be accrued to them should Atahualpa be successful in his bid for power.

One final twist in the tale remained before all-out conflict broke out between the brothers. The Cañari – fierce warriors from the lowlands east of Quito, but lately incorporated into the Inca Empire – took advantage of the incipient chaos in this Andean realm and captured Atahualpa, perhaps even nominally, in the name of Huascar. The Cañari, together with the Chachapoya, served under Huascar and composed part of his personal guard, much to the annoyance of the other *panacas* of Cuzco, who had often been called upon to fulfil that privileged role. The Cañari held on to Atahualpa for a while before he escaped (losing part of his ear in the process – a significant injury given the high status earspools that the elite males wore). Atahualpa's self-mythologizing told his Spanish interrogators following his capture in 1532 that the Sun magically turned him into a snake or a mouse, thus enabling him to escape. This capture event might have delayed the marshalling of Atahualpa's forces such that he was only ready to take the war to his brother in 1529, four years after the death of their father Huayna Cápac, thereby setting the scene for the Inca Empire's descent into civil war and anarchy that would last until Atahualpa defeated Huascar on the eve of Spanish arrival in 1532. What emerged from this period of intercine warfare would be a very different world.

Before the start of the civil war, Huascar had already managed to enrage his local base in Cuzco: first, by changing the composition of his guard of Incas from royal households to foreigners; second, by failing to attend the great feasts and bacchanalia of the *panacas* and *ayllus* held all too frequently in the plazas of Cuzco. These occasions were crucial for re-energizing the reciprocal ties between ruler and ruled – especially important in the context of the Andes where ties of reciprocity were what held the fabric of society together. Huascar's lack of engagement might indicate a failure of character, or perhaps a wider strategy to bring the *panacas* to heel. The *panacas* were based around the veneration of deceased *sapa* Incas. Furthermore, the Inca practice of split inheritance, where the dead Inca retained his lands and household, while his heir gained the throne and little else, meant that a number of these *panacas* had control over the best lands and resources, especially in and around Cuzco. These dead ancestors and their households also tended to flex their political muscle in the regular councils with the *sapa* Inca; for instance, being able to counter and enforce their alternatives on decisions arrived at by the living *sapa* Inca.

In this sense, while Atahualpa donned the traditionalist mantle, ostensibly seeking to respect the rights and privileges of the *panacas*, Huascar played the role of the iconoclast, threatening to expropriate their lands, bury the ancestral Inca mummies – thus curtailing their veneration – while moving actively to disband the royal households. He also toyed with the idea of shifting the Inca rulership from its traditional upper (*hanan*) Cuzco base to that of lower (*hurin*) Cuzco, thereby potentially effecting a dramatic shift in political power within the city and state. What at any other time might have been construed as an ambitious programme of political and social renewal, was a singularly dangerous ploy in the face of a strong alternative rival for the throne. What's more, Atahualpa's own powerful Hatun *panaca* of his great-grandfather Pachacutec Inca Yupanqui acted as a veritable fifth column within Cuzco, garnering increasing support from *panacas* disaffected and disgruntled by Huascar's reformist ideas and actions.

Even so, had Huascar been a more astute, or a luckier, general, he could have gotten away with it. As it was, however, failure in the field of battle meant that the powder keg of courtly intrigue undermined him, and sealed the fate of his family and household. In matters of war, with his father's veteran armies and victorious generals Atahualpa had a singular advantage. However, early on he could only count on the backing of part of the Chinchaysuyu region, essentially from northern Peru and Ecuador; he still had to contend against the rest of the Inca state. That said, Huascar seems to have been slow on the uptake, such that while he could count on meagre troops from the small eastern quarter, the Antisuyu, and the equally small central coastal quarter, the Cuntinsuyu, troops from the larger, more sparse southern Collasuyu were slow in being mustered. As such, both factions mainly drew their levies from the populous Chinchaysuyu quarter, making this very much a conflict of the Central Andean region.

The first major battle between the factions occurred near Tumipampa, the site of Ninan Cuyuchi's death. On the field of Chillopampa, Huascar's generals Atoc and Hango, carrying an effigy of the Sun, faced off against Atahualpan generals Chalcochima and Quizquiz. After initial success on the battlefield by Huascar's faction, Chalcochima managed to turn the tide at the subsequent battle at Mullihambato alongside the Ambato River. At this second battle, Ullco Cola, the lord of Tumipampa, was captured and killed. Also captured were Atoc and Hongo. Their skins were flayed and turned into drums, and Atoc's skull was turned into a gold-plated cup that Atahualpa used for drinking *chicha* (maize beer). The family of Ullco Cola were slaughtered, setting a standard of cruelty that underscored this increasingly bitter conflict. Atahualpa later punished Huascar's northern allies, the Cañari and Chachapoya, most severely, both for the former's capture of him and their continued loyalty to his half-brother. In turn, this revenge made early Spanish allies of these two ethnic groups. It was at Tumipampa that Atahualpa officially accepted the *mascaipacha* and Inca rulership.

After these initial battles, several erstwhile allies of Huascar switched sides to Atahualpa, expanding his power base. Atahualpa and his generals continued southwards, now fighting against Huascar's new quadrumvirate of generals: Guanca Auqui, Ahuapanti, Urco Guaranca and Inca Roca. A series of encounters at Caxabamba, Cocha Guailla, Pumpu, Jauja and Vilcas went badly for the Cuzco armies, with Atahualpa heaping defeat on defeat against Huascar's ever retreating host while gaining new adherents to his cause. It seems that the expertise and battle prowess of Atahualpa's troops and generals more than compensated for their lesser numbers. Throughout these engagements, Atahualpa had remained aloof yet informed of the proceedings, preferring his generals to pursue the battles rather than to attend to them personally.

Finally cornered, Huascar himself took to the field and offered battle at Tambobamba on the Apurimac River near to Cuzco. During the event, an overly complex converging strategy by Huascar, involving three separate armies, and his military inexperience proved to be his undoing. The wannabe Cuzco-led ambushers were, in turn, ambushed, with Huascar and his principal general Guanca Auqui captured by Chalcochima, Quizquiz and their victorious troops. The defeated were paraded into Cuzco, where all the *panacas* and principal denizens of the city were made to pay their respects to Atahualpa's 'brother' or second, his *huauque* effigy known as Ticsi Capac, which at times such as this personified Atahualpa himself. News of this victory and the end of the war was sent to Atahualpa, at the time residing in Huamachuco, in the north of modern-day Peru.

Meanwhile, the time for revenge had come. Following Atahualpa's capture of Cuzco, Huascar's last general – Guanca Auqui – was put to death, as were Apo Challco Yupanqui and Rupaca, the Sun priests that had crowned Huascar. But this was just the beginning. At this time, Cusi Topa Yupanqui arrived, the same individual tasked with conveying the news to Atahualpa of his father's death back in 1525. A member of Pachacutec's Hatun *panaca* – kinsman to Atahualpa's mother, and therefore to Atahualpa himself – Cusi Topa Yupanqui was an early convert to Atahualpa's cause, and his role in Cuzco during 1532 was to mete out punishment to Huascar's kin. All members of Topa Inca Yupanqui's *panaca*, Huascar's mother's household, were targeted for extermination, as was Huascar's extended family. All were hanged, including their *yanacona* servants. Additionally, in an extreme act of iconoclasm, the venerated and sacred mummy of Topa Inca Yupanqui himself was burnt and destroyed.

This last act was exceptional, as the destruction of Topa Inca Yupanqui's remains effectively ended his household. It might also have been a preliminary step towards reorganizing Cuzco's politics. By having over eighty close kin of Huascar, including women and children, as well as descendants of Topa Inca Yupanqui – and a fair number of brothers – killed, Atahualpa seems to have been intending to found a new *panaca*, the Ticci Capac or 'New Foundation' *panaca*, which would have been associated with him personally. In this light, his actions – including the burning of Topa Inca Yupanqui's mummy, his *quipu* and the destruction of his household – suggest that Atahualpa might have been attempting to rewrite history, possibly in a similar fashion to Pachucutec three generations before. The burning of Topa Inca Yupanqui's *quipu* in effect meant the erasing of this *sapa* Inca's history. It is intriguing to imagine what might have happened to Inca historiography had Atahualpa managed to enact these changes; perhaps Topa Inca Yupanqui's *panaca* would have disappeared, and with it his place in the history of Inca expansion.

Few of Huascar's family survived the slaughter, although crucially his half-brothers Manco Inca and Paullu Inca did. Manco Inca escaped the Cuzco purge dressed as a peasant, and hid himself in the immediacy of the capital, while Paullu Inca fled to his power base in the Collao near Lake Titicaca. These two brothers would shape subsequent Inca responses to the arrival of the Spanish, with Manco Capac, known as Manco Inca, initially siding with, even serving as a puppet Inca for, the Europeans, before rebelling against them. Paullu Inca would in turn become an ardent supporter of the Spaniards. Their descendants would likewise pick their respective fathers' sides in the Inca's final chapter in the Andes.

By all accounts, both sides in the civil war managed to amass formidable forces to face each other, numbering in the thousands and possibly in the hundreds of thousands. Yet what was the composition of these troops, and how were they organized for battle? Aside from a small corps of professional warriors that accompanied and formed the Inca's personal guard, most Inca troops were levied from the local peasantry as part of their *mit'a* labour obligations to the state. The professional corps of guard troops was usually made up of Inca nobles, or *orejones* (large-eared ones), so named for the large spools they placed in their ears as an insignia of social rank. It became increasingly common for the *sapa* Inca to supplement these Inca nobles with warriors from other ethnic groups. Given the propensity for royal Inca, from which the *orejones* were chosen, to root for their household, this is perhaps not surprising. Huascar seems to have taken this to its logical conclusion and excluded most of the *orejones* from his guard corps, ruffling feathers among the Cuzco elite.

The rest of the warriors were levied from their constituent communities, often serving under their local chiefs. This, coupled with the plethora of local languages and dialects, made Inca armies unwieldy, although beautifully pageanted, with each individual group carrying their distinct clothes and insignia. In battle they were arrayed into incremental decimal groups of 10, 100, 1,000 and 10,000, each subdivided into two and led by their respective leaders. It is likely that these troops would have been rudimentarily drilled under this command structure to make these sizable bodies of men manageable in battle. This dualistic division of command and control extended to the ranks of generals, so that each and every army invariably had two, or sometimes even four, generals leading them. Although it is hard to verify the number of soldiers in Inca armies, especially given Spanish witnesses' propensity to exaggerate the numbers faced by their compatriots, there still seem to have been large contingents of up to, and sometimes surpassing, 100,000 troops. At the Siege of Cuzco in 1536, Manco Inca amassed a truly huge army of between 100,000 and 200,000 warriors, and during the Inca Civil War both Huascar and Atahualpa regularly fielded armies of more than 100,000 men, even if their usual strength at the point of battle was between 30,000 and 50,000 effectives.

The lack of large draught animals also meant that it was a slow-moving army with large contingents of porters, camelid herders, wives and servants making a veritable second army of auxiliaries accompanying the troops. A good daily rate of movement would have been 15 to 20 kilometres (9–12 mi.) between the larger staging posts along the main Inca road system. By way of comparison, the Roman Army – excluding cavalry – during the third century AD moved on average 30 kilometres (18 mi.) a day and between 40 and 45 kilometres (25–8 mi.) a day on a forced march; Inca armies were slow. Central to these armies progress was the vast Inca road network or Capac Ñan. This was the nodal system on which these armies moved and replenished themselves, using the storage facilities built along the way for just this purpose. As the empire expanded, the need for greater scope and professionalism in the army grew apace. The use and implantation of colonists (*mitma*) in particularly recalcitrant regions meant that a cadre of supposedly loyal troops were always at hand in case of trouble. Additionally, a series of forts along the southern and eastern frontiers of the empire served as an early warning system against incursions from afar, in a fashion similar to that of Hadrian's Wall in Britain or the Roman *limes* along the line of the Rhine and Danube.

The lack of iron technology meant that the available weaponry was predominantly wood and stone based, with bolas, slingshot, clubs and maces being particularly favoured. Bronze was also used to make star-shaped or rounded mace heads. All in all, the military hardware was primordially of the blunt variety and armour was

Star-shaped Inca macehead, Viejo Sangayaico, Huancavelica, Peru.

of quilted cotton or leather, augmented with metal plates, wood and cane. Concussion damage was therefore the most common injury sustained in Andean combat. Spears and obsidian-tipped arrows were also used, the latter being especially the preserve of Antisuyu jungle warriors, who also employed darts of different kinds. Fighting was mostly hand-to-hand and was preceded by chanting, singing, insults and confrontational bravado which could sometimes go on for days. This ritualized initiation to combat was quickly discarded by the Inca when the Spanish patently did not enjoin in the proceedings, but rather benefitted from these preliminaries to swiftly inflict defeat or gain advantage over their enemies. Likewise, the Inca tended not to attack on a new moon, which was reserved for sacred ceremonies to Mama Quilla, the Moon, a further advantage that the Spanish exploited, for instance, against Manco Inca's fortified position above Cuzco at Sacsahuamán during the siege of the city.

There were no siege weapons to speak off, so assaults on heavily defended hilltop forts were conducted either through subterfuge or full-frontal assault. In turn, besieged troops often used rolling boulders to dislodge incoming attacks. The use of boulders, this time on narrow mountain passes, would be a tactic often utilized by the Inca and their indigenous allies against Spanish troops. Memorably, Gonzalo de Tapia's and Diego Pizarro's contingents of seventy and sixty horsemen, respectively, were ambushed and destroyed by the Inca general Quizo Yupanqui as they marched to relieve the Manco Inca's siege of Spanish-held Cuzco in 1536. In battles conducted in the open, indigenous fighting descended into large melees with feints and flanking manoeuvres employed to disorientate and unbalance the enemy.

Unfortunately, the Inca tended to lead from the front; not a problem when the enemy had the same general level of technology and, in particular, reach, but a flawed tactic against steel-armed, harquebus-wielding Spanish footmen and horsemen. At the Battle of Lima in 1536, after successfully occupying the high ground around Cerro San Cristóbal, the same triumphant boulder ambush general – Quizo Yupanqui – decided to offer pitched battle in typical Andean style against the Spanish in the town. This was a fateful mistake. Leading from the front, Quizo Yupanqui and forty other commanders were quickly massacred, and his army, thus bereft of leadership, routed. Indeed, the overtly vertical leadership structure of Inca command often meant that the capture of generals, or the *sapa* Inca himself, could paralyse an army or faction. Huascar's capture in 1532 by Atahualpa's troops effectively eliminated him as a threat. Similarly, Atahualpa's capture by the Spanish that same year tragically immobilized his armies at a time when the Spanish were still weak and seriously outnumbered in the Andes.

Ritual and ceremony were never far from the army and military campaigns. Before setting off on campaign or prior to battle, animal – or even human – sacrifices (*capacocha*) were conducted and *huacas* (a spirit or deity revealed in an object, feature or as a natural phenomenon, with oracular powers) consulted. The more powerful the *huaca*, the more potent its advice. Sometimes, though, the oracle did not tell you what you wanted to hear. When

The Inca redoubt of Sacsahuamán above Cuzco.

Atahualpa sought out Catequil, a famous central Andean *huaca*, for advice, Catequil predicted that he would not be successful in his endeavours. Atahualpa had the temple destroyed and razed to the ground and its high priest killed. In this case, however, Catequil was ultimately proven correct. Important icons and effigies of *huacas*, the Sun (*Inti*) and thunder (*Illapa*) were carried into battle, while capture and hostage-taking of an enemy's *huacas* was a potent symbol of victory and subjugation.

Ultimately, Inca militarism was much more focused on strategy and logistics than battlefield tactics, training or technology. Aside from the elite corps around the Inca, the mostly levied troops were raised during the fallow period following the harvest and then marched out. This meant that, aside from the disruptive civil war when both Huascar and Atahualpa fought outside the normal yearly time frame for raising troops, military campaigns were mainly limited to between the months of March and July. Manco Inca's attempt to recapture Spanish-held Cuzco in 1536 came to nothing when his army dissipated during August–September, needing to plant the year's new crops. It also meant

that these troops were hardly professional armies; in most cases they were ordinary farmers and herders with rudimentary training and expertise, or with fighting skills more adapted to the incessant raiding that seems to have been the mainstay of Andean highland conflict prior to the rise of the Inca. There were exceptions to this, with certain ethnic groups furnishing better trained and bellicose warriors; this certainly seems to have been the case with Atahualpa's troops. Huascar's armies, in contrast – though numerous and spectacular – were less well trained and battle-ready. They suffered tremendously because of these deficiencies.

These varied disadvantages among their armies meant that more often than not the Inca sought alliances, rather than conflict, as a means to expand the empire. War was then reserved for particularly stubborn foes, such as the tribes along the northern, southern and eastern fringes of the empire, or the kingdom of Chimor. Chimor, on the northern Peruvian coast, was easily the most advanced and sophisticated entity that the Inca faced in their successful rise to empire. At its largest extent, Chimor covered an area of land stretching from the modern-day border with Ecuador southwards almost to Lima itself. There was no possibility of accommodation between these two expansionist states, and after a long and arduous series of campaigns that straddled the reigns of Pachacutec and Topa Inca Yupanqui, the Chimor were defeated, and their last leader, or Gran Chimú, Minchancaman, was brought to Cuzco with his *huacas* as hostages. The Inca also appropriated Chimor's coveted metalworking artisans for their own uses. Minchancaman's defeated kingdom was then reduced to the status of vassalage under the leadership of Chumun Caur. Interestingly, conquest of Chimor was effected through a combination of battle and the ploy of destroying Chimor's access to water supplies from the highlands. This last tactic was probably part of a tried and tested stratagem against coastal cultures. Based on the water-parched coast, Chimor was always going to suffer hardship from disruption to this essential resource.

Conquest of Chimor made groups formerly allied to them switch their allegiance to the Inca without the need for extra war campaigning. Ultimately, though, the many myriad alliances that held the weft and warp of the empire together were only ever as strong as the Inca that commanded the different groups' loyalties. In the increasingly frayed political setting following the death of Huayna Cápac and the Inca Civil War, these loyalties were tested to the limit. Into this emergent vacuum came first pestilence and then the Spanish.

Francisco Pizarro (1475–1541) and his 167 followers did not defeat the Inca Empire; it was already teetering at the beginning of the 1530s, and Spanish entry was the straw that broke the camel's back. Even before the Inca Civil War, European disease and epidemics had ravaged the Andes, causing widespread anguish and depression among the indigenous populations. After millennia of isolation, indigenous Americans had precious little immunity to Old World diseases. It is important, then, to understand the background in which these pandemics hit the Andes, and how they were interpreted by the locals, to fully appreciate the very real impact they must have had on the indigenous inhabitants. In a context where modern medicine and appreciation of viruses, germs and disease were rudimentary to say the least, this influx of deadly new illnesses was extremely distressing, as they are indeed still in the recent context of COVID-19.

During the early Spanish colony, indigenous witnesses to this period spoke of a pall hanging over large areas of the Andes, and of ill-portents signalling the demise of the Inca. While they can be read as a post-event, justification for the approaching apocalypse, it is also obvious that a miasma of disease was patently present across the empire. For instance, the first epidemic, smallpox (1524–5), claimed an estimated 48 per cent of the population, including, as previously mentioned, the ruling Inca and his designated heir. Indeed, the incipient urbanization of large areas of the Inca Empire and their own 'royal road', the Capac Ñan, aided the swift spread of disease vectors throughout the land. Smallpox struck again twice during the 1530s, when Manco Inca and his allies were fighting for the survival of their way of life and style of government. Smallpox hit again in 1557, 1566, 1582 and 1585, interspersed with measles, typhus, pneumonic plague, influenza and mumps, to name a few. A veritable cocktail of death. While the Spanish were hardly immune to these diseases, they did have a greater tolerance of them. It must have dispirited the local populations immensely to face an invisible enemy that spared (in large part) the Spanish but decimated their own ranks. The grim tally speaks for itself; it is estimated that by the end of the sixteenth century, less than eighty years after these illnesses first appeared, nine out of ten people among the local population had succumbed. By the early seventeenth century there were barely 1 million indigenous people in the Andean region, an area that had previously held a population of between 12 and 15 million in its Inca heyday.

The backdrop was one of populational and cultural crisis for the Inca, and indeed for the larger indigenous population. This is reflected in the early Spanish Cuzco School of Art, which was composed, in the main, of indigenous painters and sculptors who adopted the Tenebrist Baroque style of light and shadow favoured by Peninsular artists such as Francisco de Zurbarán (1598–1664) and Diego Velázquez (1599–1660). They adopted this art style because it was in vogue, but also due to its dark undertones and themes. Early Christ and martyred saint sculptures depict pale, overly gaunt, almost sickly figures, often awash in blood. It is tempting to see this very much as art imitating life, in a world where morbidity was spiking alarmingly, and people were dying from terrifying new illnesses. At such a time, this darker artistic interpretation must have appealed to indigenous sensibilities. On the wider matter of religion, the image of Jesus Christ as a living-in-death figure must have also particularly appealed to Andean people and their penchant for ancestor worship.

Therefore, aside from the truly audacious initial attack on Atahualpa and his entourage at Cajamarca on that fateful morning of 16 November 1532, the Spaniards led by Francisco Pizarro did not by themselves topple the empire. Furthermore, alongside epidemics and disease, they could always count on allies among the disaffected indigenous groups. These ranged from the Cañari and Chachapoya in the north, the Chimor on the coast and the Huanca and Chanca in the Central Andes. Inca factions, or *panacas*, also allied themselves with the Spanish conquistadors, crucially including Paullu Inca, another scion of Huayna Cápac.

That said, the capture of Atahualpa by the Spanish at Cajamarca changed the rules of engagement. The vertical nature of the Inca rule meant that with Atahualpa's capture, Inca leadership was effectively paralysed. Atahualpa's precipitate execution of his former rival Huascar, while he himself was captive, eliminated an obvious candidate around which Inca resistance could have coalesced, and was a grave misreading of the Spanish and their long-term intentions. These intentions were nothing less than the subjugation of the Inca Empire. Atahualpa offered a massive ransom in silver and gold, which the Spaniards accepted: both biding their time, both hoping to squeeze some advantage out of the situation. Yet prevarication was in the Spanish interest. The ransom's collection allowed the conquistadors to scout large areas of the empire, including Cuzco itself, and provided time for new reinforcements to arrive. This initially included Diego de Almagro (1475–1538), Francisco Pizarro's partner on this endeavour, and 150 extra men, although further soldiers and adventurers from Central America were not long in arriving.

As an aside, crucial to Diego de Almagro's reinforcements were the fifty horses and horsemen he brought with him. Horses did not exist in the Andes prior to the arrival of the Spanish, and

Manco Inca, *sapa* Inca in Vilcabamba, from Poma de Ayala, *Nueva corónica y buen gobierno* (1615).

horsemen's presence in battle had a disproportionate impact to their paltry numbers. In early encounters with them, the Inca simply did not know how to deal with them. Cavalry charges by coordinated groups of Spanish horsemen were enough to induce outright panic in indigenous forces, leading to numerous massacres and slaughters. Small wonder that a horseman was paid upwards of ten times what a footman earned from the loot at Cajamarca. Initially, Andean people thought that the rider and horse were one single entity. Furthermore, the bit between the teeth of the horses was interpreted by the indigenous population as proof that horses ate metal, an idea that was encouraged by the Spanish as it made the horse seem more ferocious and lent substance to their constant appeals for precious metals. Indeed, when Hernando Pizarro (Francisco Pizarro's half-brother) came to the coastal oracle of Pachacamac, determined to loot it, he hid corn among some silver and gold on the floor to show that the horses were eating metal, and that therefore the temple had to be stripped to feed these partially metal-caparisoned beasts.

Returning to Cajamarca and Atahualpa's imprisonment, Francisco Pizarro also used this time to sound out indigenous leaders and potential allies, so that following the Inca's execution on trumped up charges the army that left Cajamarca in 1533 was a hybrid Hispano–indigenous force. By then, the Spanish had offered the *mascaipacha* to the first in a string of Inca puppet rulers, in this case Túpac Hualpa, or Toparpa, a son of Huayna Cápac by his wife Mama Palla Chimpu Tucto Coca. He lasted only a few months in this role and died en route to Cuzco, possibly poisoned by the Atahualpan general Chalcochima, who was by then also a captive of the Spanish. The next puppet Inca was Manco Inca (1516–1544), yet another son of Huayna Cápac and a survivor of Atahualpa's purge of Huascar's kin.

Information from several sources seem to indicate that Manco Inca selected as co-ruler his brother Paullu Inca (1518–1549), fulfilling many of the duties and obligations of the role similar to Topa Amaru alongside Pachacutec Inca Yupanqui in the fifteenth century. In normal circumstances Paullu Inca (later Cristóbal Paullu Inca, after he was baptised) would not have been considered a first-line candidate for co-rulership, or the *mascaipacha*, in his own right, given that he was the son of Huayna Cápac and his marriage to the daughter of the *cacique* or lord of Guaillas (Huaylas), Añaz Colque. He therefore had no matrilineal *panaca*

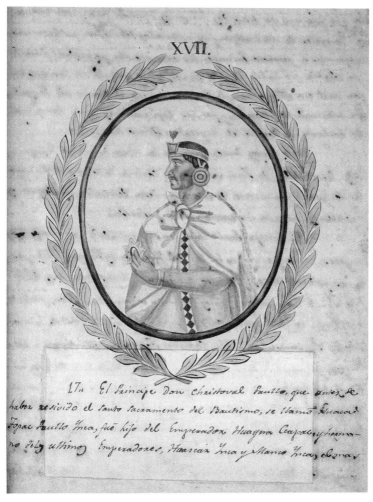

Don Cristóbal Paullu Inca, *sapa* Inca in Spanish Cuzco, from Justo Apu Sahuaraura Inca's manuscript 'Recuerdos de la monarquía peruana, ó, Bosquejo de la historia de los incas' (1838).

to back him in Cuzco. Paullu Inca's marriage to Tocto Ussica, a daughter of Huayna Cápac and therefore his half-sister (she was also a descendant of Inca Roca), meant that her *panaca* lent some belated legitimacy to his claim, but the fact remains that he could only have aspired to the throne in the turbulent atmosphere existing after the extensive purges of the civil war and the generalized collapse of Inca statehood that followed the Spanish invasion.

John Everett Millais, *Pizarro Seizing the Inca of Peru*, 1846, oil on canvas.

These two individuals, Manco Inca and Paullu Inca, were to set the tone for the varied Inca response to Spanish conquest of the Andes. Manco Inca was the Spaniards' puppet Inca for only two years, and in 1536 he raised the banner of rebellion against the Spanish. In the meantime, his brother Paullu Inca was away campaigning on Manco Inca's and Spanish behalf in the extensive southern Collasuyu. Manco Inca's great revolt spanned two years (1535–7) before his inability to take Cuzco or Lima, or eradicate the Spanish and their allies, condemned it to failure. Lima, known officially as the Ciudad de los Reyes, or 'city of kings', became the new fledgling capital of this soon-to-be Spanish viceroyalty of Peru (established in 1542). A second rebellion by Manco Inca in 1539 also came to naught. By then, chastised and almost captured himself, he had fled to Vilcabamba in the humid cloud-forest lowlands, some 150 kilometres (90 mi.) to the northwest of Cuzco. There he established a nascent neo-Inca state that was to survive through him and the rule of three of his sons until 1572.

It was Paullu Inca's return accompanying the Spanish troops of Diego de Almagro that convinced Manco Inca to abandon his siege of Cuzco in 1537 and flee to his forest redoubt in Vilcabamba.

Quickly appraising the situation, and already having proved his loyalty and worth to the Spanish, Paullu Inca stepped into the vacuum left by his brother and seized the *mascaipacha* himself. In so doing, Paullu Inca did what every effective Inca had always done: favour his faction. In this he was singularly successful, at least until his grandson, Melchor Carlos Inca (1574–1610), dissipated his considerable inheritance. In contrast to Manco Inca, Paullu Inca took the path of accommodation, and reaped the reward that this loyalty brought with it. It would be easy to condemn Paullu Inca as a base traitor to his people, but this revisionism flies in the face of the very real sorrow and lamentation among the indigenous nobles and commoners of Cuzco that accompanied his funeral cortège in 1544. He made a choice, as Manco Inca did, and many of his people followed him. Subsequent history might have vilified him, but at the time many of his compatriots would have agreed with his decision.

That said, the death knell to the Inca Empire as an independent indigenous entity had come earlier: it had been sounded by the brutal campaign that pitted the Atahualpan North against the Huascan South, leading to the complete disruption of Inca imperial organization as province turned against province, and the administration lapsed under the pressures of civil war. Against this backdrop of conflict there was the added misery of disease. It was precisely at this moment in May 1532, when Atahualpa emerged victorious over Huascar, that Francisco Pizarro landed in Tumbes, northern Peru. Although rebellion, conflict and possibly civil war had been a staple of Inca succession crises going back down the regal line, this time the arrival of the Spanish made everything different. In this case, a weakened empire riven by a recent fratricidal war, a flagging economy, administration, disease and the loss of control over provinces was the perfect storm. With it the fate of an empire was sealed, and the rest, as they say, is history.

EIGHT

THE PAST IN THE PRESENT

Was the Indian happy? It must be supposed that he was, since he yearns for the past with so much ardour.

LOUIS BAUDIN, *A Socialist Empire: The Incas of Peru* (1961)

Traditionally the debacle of 1532 is seen as the end of the Inca Empire, and while in large measure that is true, it is not quite the complete story. As we mentioned in the Preface, while the Inca may be considered a prehistoric – or at most a protohistoric – culture, its collapse in the face of European colonization within the last five hundred years means two things. The first is that we can access this culture far more vividly than other protohistoric cultures, having access through ethnohistoric and early historical writings of the people that occupied and lived in this newly conquered Andean zone. This is not the case with the majority of prehistoric cultures, even the protohistoric ones of Iron Age Europe (*c.* 1200 BC–AD 50), which were often known only very tangentially through classical writers. The amount of information available is also of a different magnitude. The availability of this information is basically a question of preservation: quite simply, there are a lot more texts in existence from the sixteenth and seventeenth centuries AD than from the first century AD or earlier.

The second major factor that comes into play when analysing the Inca is that their demise did not mean the end of an Andean way of life. In this sense, while Andean culture was much changed and hybridized by its contact with Spanish colonization, it did remain a living culture as opposed to a dead one, such as those of the ancient Greeks or Romans. The persistence and survival of

Andean culture through extreme stress and hardship is attested by the often superb ethnographies on the Andes that exist, and by the mere physical presence of indigenous communities along the length and breadth of the Andes, especially in the highlands. Modern tourism to Andean countries makes much play of this authenticity, even if it has been irrevocably changed and altered by almost five hundred years of European contact.

Nevertheless, we should not underestimate the severe disruption and dislocation that occurred. Indeed, it is a measure of how dramatic the impact of European colonization in South America was that the Inca, and coeval ethnic groups such as the Chimor, Huaylas, Chanca and so on, remain inadequately known (even though some documents on Chimor and others, including dynastic lists, do exist), with most of our knowledge gleaned from archaeology rather than history. The population decline was too steep (reducing the number of potential interviewees of past events within a very short time span), and Spanish interest in the minutiae of indigenous lifeways too sparse, to make more than a mere indent into the vast panorama of Andean and Inca culture history. Adding to this, the largely indecipherable nature of the knotted-string 'written' language of the Inca *quipu* means that our historical understanding of the Andes is reduced essentially to the 100–150 years prior to European contact. In essence, this means that it was still possible in the early sixteenth century for Spanish chroniclers to interview indigenous witnesses with folk memory and stories pertaining to this period of a century or so prior to Spanish arrival in the Andes in 1532. From a historical perspective, tracing the development of Andean culture even further back becomes increasingly more nerve-wracking and subjective. It is at this point that archaeology becomes our first tool of choice in filling in the yawning gaps that exist in our knowledge of these more remote times.

Spanish colonization of South America was not a one-way affair. This transcontinental transfer known as the Columbian Exchange ranged from diseases to crops and animals, and completely transformed the world leading to the first real globalization. Nowadays it would be impossible to think of certain country-specific cuisines without tomatoes or chillies, yet they came from the Americas. More specifically, potatoes, the fourth-largest world staple crop, were domesticated in the Andean region. Maize too made a gigantic contribution to global household economies, as has squash, beans and peanuts. Nevertheless, European products also brought benefits to indigenous populations. They received, for instance, wheat and rice, as well as grapes, olives and bananas.

Yet perhaps the greatest change was in respect to animals. South America had few large ungulates, and although two of these – alpacas and vicuñas – provided some of the finest natural fibres known to mankind, the Old World had many other animals, including cows, pigs, goats and sheep. All these creatures reproduced quicker and provided more milk, meat and wool respectively than native American animals. Also, Old World pack animals were of a different order to the low-load-carrying llama. Horses, mules, donkeys and asses revolutionized travel, message-carrying and portage throughout the Americas. In turn, this meant that it was in Spanish interests to maintain large segments of the Inca road system – the Capac Ñan – especially the *tampu*, or inns, as the arteries connecting their newly founded viceroyalty. This ensured the survival of large tracts of the Capac Ñan – now the *Camino Real*, or Royal Road – well into the early twentieth century.

On the matter of horses, so well-adapted did some indigenous South American groups, for instance the Mapuche, become to them and their use that they developed into fearsome horsemen in their own right. The Mapuche were only finally subdued in the early twentieth century, when they were comprehensively defeated and forcibly assimilated into the Chilean state. Much like their homologous Great Plains North American cousins, such as the Cheyenne, Comanche or Sioux, it is hard to explain these groups without reference to the intrinsic value horses held for their respective cultures. A value that transcended the purely functional, horse riding and the raiding and hunting that went with it became for these cultures an important element of the transition to manhood and prestige. An incredible cultural development when one considers that domesticated horses had only been introduced to the Americas in the late fifteenth century.

While the types of produce grown and livestock reared in South America changed drastically with European contact, the rhythm of communal life – what the nineteenth-century Spanish philosopher Miguel de Unamuno (1864–1936) termed 'the silent life of millions of men without history' – continued unabated, especially in the highlands. It is important to make a distinction between the coast and the highlands. Spain was an oceanic empire, and as such indigenous populations on the coast suffered first and faster changes than those in the highlands. Indigenous Andean populations tended to persist, including retaining use of their native languages, especially Quechua and Aymara, and eventually slowly recovering in the nineteenth and twentieth centuries in the more secluded highlands. Here, changes in land tenure and settlement location by the Spanish – such as the *reducciones*, literally meaning 'reductions' – where indigenous populations were resettled in, or reduced to, new colonial towns, were often passively resisted, such that the pre-Hispanic dispersed settlement pattern of households dotting the landscape continued. Sometimes they combined their main house in the fields with a smaller temporary house in the new towns which they used when they needed to engage with Spanish colonial authorities, such as for census, marriages, deaths, and so on.

While certain Inca and Andean institutions disappeared or became subsumed within the larger Spanish colonial superstructure, others were subverted by the Spanish. For instance, Inca *mitma* colonists in most cases packed-up and returned to their parent communities, especially if the displacement had happened within living memory. The community established around the *ayllu* was a powerful organization that continued to be a referent of local authority. Meanwhile, the *mit'a*, the local service obligation to the Inca state, was adopted wholesale by the Spanish – but now referred to as *mita*. The *mita* was used by colonial authorities in a variety of different ways as a form of community tax for state-sanctioned work, including infrastructure, agriculture and, most importantly, mining. From the very beginning the *mita* impositions on local populations were high, and it only became more intolerable with time. It was one of the major contributing factors behind the intermittent rebellions and revolts against colonial rule, especially during the fraught eighteenth century.

The Spanish mining *mita* was the harshest of state obligations, and the most resented. Two mines in particular captured most people's imagination then and now: the silver mine at Potosí (Bolivia) and the mercury mine at Huancavelica (Peru). These were the two biggest mining enterprises during the early Spanish colony in South America, but numerous smaller ones dotted the Andean highlands. Conditions at both were atrocious, with the life-expectancy for long-term workers remaining significantly less than forty years for the centuries that they were in use. Indeed, so bad were conditions at the Santa Barbara mercury mine at Huancavelica that it earned the sobriquet 'mine of death'. Here, mining of poisonous *llimpi*, or cinnabar (mercuric sulphide), used in the silver amalgamation process in Potosí, meant that working at the mine for only six months was a virtual death sentence owing to mercury exposure. *Mita* obligations at Huancavelica usually lasted a year. Some communities would cripple their sons, intentionally chopping off a hand in a bid to avoid the Spanish mine *mita*.

The institution of Andean religious practice also survived, adapting to the imposition of Christianity. In this sphere, even from the very beginning, resistance, revindication and continuation of Inca or indigenous worldviews and systems persisted. Once again, the survival of the old ways was always easier in the less accessible highlands. Here, alongside the neo-Inca state at Vilcabamba (1537–71), possibly the biggest threat to the early Spanish colony was the religious revivalist Taqui Ongoy movement (*c.* 1564–*c.* 1572). Through the Taqui Ongoy, disillusioned and disaffected local community members yearned for a return to their past and with it to the deities and spirits incarnate in their multiple *huacas*. Given that by this stage many god effigies, temples, amulets and shrines had been destroyed, and their attendants dispersed, the *huacas* were said to present themselves through the physical possession of individual people, among other manifestations. Thus embodied, the *huacas* called for a return to the old religion and instigated people to dance to bring on renewal. In fact, Taqui Ongoy can be loosely translated as 'the dancing sickness', and was oddly reminiscent of the Ghost Dance of the indigenous North Americans, at the end of the nineteenth century, where similarly dancing was the medium through which the end of days would arrive, bringing with it an indigenous rebirth. Such millennialist movements were a common enough occurrence among many other indigenous cultures under the oppression of colonial rule. The Taqui Ongoys believed that dancing and sacrifices would allow the *huacas* to bring down divine retribution on the Spanish and their local lackeys, sweeping them all away into the sea while presaging a return to the old ways.

The authorities were concerned enough to take this matter seriously and it was one of the principal reasons behind the creation of the *Extirpación de Idolatrías* (Extirpation of Idolatries) by the Spanish colonial government. Known as the bastard daughter of the Spanish Inquisition, these were state-sanctioned pogroms focused on seeking out and destroying idols, temples and all the paraphernalia of Andean religion, as well as ridding communities of indigenous priests and priestesses. Interestingly, these pogroms, repression and eventual compromises led to Andean beliefs being subsumed within Christianity, creating a curious syncretic mix in which Christian saints often replaced Andean deities, yet complete with their *huaca* powers. In this manner, the famous oracle of Pachacamac on the central Peruvian coast became the Christ figure of the *Señor de los Milagros* (Lord of Miracles), able to abate earthquakes and protect the vulnerable. Lightning, venerated through the Andean highlands as one of the most powerful of earthly deities, became Santiago *mata Moros* or *mata Indios* (St James Moor or Indian killer). Santiago was typically depicted on a horse trampling infidels, or 'Indians', while carrying a spear. The spear acted as a useful prop for lightning in the Andean imagination, hence this saint's attribution to the indigenous lightning deity. Additionally, at the time of conquest, 'Santiago' was the Spanish battle cry employed when attacking. This, combined with their discharging of cannon and arquebuses, must have seemed to the indigenous population like a true manifestation of Illapa, thereby contributing to Santiago's later easy association with thunder and lightning. Furthermore, mirroring the Andean lightning

Statue of Santiago *mata Indios* outside the Iglesia de la Compañía de Jesús, Plaza de Armas, Cusco.

god-head, Santiago was, and still is, the patron saint of herds and purveyor of water for harvests.

In the end, syncretism and hybridity were always going to be the halfway house where the indigenous pushback against alien Spanish impositions would lead to a uniquely Andean take on matters, in this case on Catholic Christianity. This syncretism still exists today, where saints and crosses jostle with sentient mountains and veneration of the *Pachamama* (Earth Mother). Indeed, it has only been the relatively recent rise of evangelical churches across South America that has instigated a serious break with local syncretic practices, leading to a move away from an Andino-Christian worship of the land and its saints and towards a stricter adherence to a remote Christian God, devoid of any peculiarly Andean connotations. Nowadays this new militant evangelism vies with Andean Christianity for the hearts, souls and minds of the indigenous people. It is still too soon to say which will hold ultimate sway, although given past Andean resilience in the face of foreign cultural onslaughts it may be that once again the indigenous, or some modification of it, will keep these new forces at bay (or modified enough to fit within an indigenous worldview).

As for the Inca themselves, they also initially survived the tumult of conquest in a variety of different ways. Inca dynastic descendants were still very present during the first few centuries of contact and into the early nineteenth century, during the struggle for independence against Spain by the Creole republics of South America. Initially this Inca survival was based on Paullu Inca (1518–1549: baptized Cristóbal Paullu Inca), Spain's puppet Inca in Cuzco, and Manco Inca (*c.* 1515–1544) in the rump independent neo-Inca state of Vilcabamba, and their respective immediate successors.

Paullu Inca's descendants quickly spent their inheritance, such that when his grandson Melchor Carlos Inca (1574–1610) died most of his wealth had been lost to feckless high-living. Tragically this last male scion of Paullu Inca left no legitimate heirs. Manco Incas's progeny initially fared somewhat better. Ensconced in their forest redoubt Manco Inca maintained a steady pressure on the still young Spanish viceroyalty. After the failure of his two rebellions, Manco Inca adapted his style of fighting, opting instead for asymmetrical warfare against the Spanish invaders. In pursuing this type of attack, the neo-Inca eschewed direct confrontation, opting instead for subterfuge and ambush, where their lack of modern weaponry was offset by an intimate knowledge of the land and their potential for surprising the enemy. Indeed, the vastness, inaccessibility and sheer ruggedness of the Andes held the key for numerous rebellions and revolutions all the way to the twentieth century.

Therefore, defeat in the 1530s did not bring the end of resistance, with first Manco Inca, and then his sons – Sayri Túpac, Titu Cusi Yupanqui and Túpac Amaru – initiating a bush war and policy of harassment against the Spanish from their centrally located Vilcabamba stronghold. While the kingdom of Vilcabamba had four different rulers, it owed its existence to the inspired leadership of Manco Inca and his son, Titu Cusi Yupanqui (1529–1571). These two individuals were willing to learn, adapt and resist Spanish presence in innovative ways. For instance, Manco Inca famously led a charge with captured horses and swords against Spanish footmen at the Battle of Ollantaytambo in 1537, routing them in the process.

In turn, Titu Cusi produced probably one of the most remarkable documents ever written on the Inca Empire. Dictated to the Spanish priest Marcos Garcia and transcribed by Titu Cusi Yupanqui's *mestizo* secretary, Martin Pando, his apologia to Philip III (1527–1598), king of Spain – entitled *History of How the Spaniards Arrived in Peru* – provides the only truly Inca perspective on the seminal events surrounding Pizarro's encounter with Atahualpa at Cajamarca in 1532, and offers a strong defence of Inca rule over the Andes. Both these Inca leaders were also adept at playing off different Spanish factions and even diplomatically toying with conversion to Christianity and emerging from the jungle, while all the time remaining in Vilcabamba. All these were ploys towards preserving the independence of their newly founded kingdom.

The other two sons were somewhat less able at keeping Spanish interests and demands at bay. Sayri Túpac (*c.* 1535–1560) capitulated to the Spanish and emerged to live in some luxury in Cuzco, but not before bequeathing Vilcabamba and the *mascaipacha* – the tasselled fringe and Inca symbol of rule – to his remarkable half-brother Titu Cusi Yupanqui. Meanwhile, Túpac Amaru (1545–1572), the last independent ruler of Vilcabamba, ill-advisedly decided to embrace a more nativist version of Inca identity, rejecting advances in warfare and the to-and-fro diplomatic game that his brother and father had so successfully employed. Unfortunately, his brief reign coincided with that of Francisco de Toledo, Count of Oropesa (1515–1582), among the more energetic and ruthless of the late sixteenth-century viceroys of Peru. Viceroy Francisco de Toledo was determined to root out Andean links to the past, both in the religious sphere, through his destruction of local *huacas*, and in the political arena, invading Vilcabamba and dragging Túpac Amaru back to Cuzco. There, a fate similar to that of his uncle Atahualpa awaited Túpac Amaru; in 1572, he was beheaded in the main plaza of the old Inca capital, his death witnessed by locals and Spaniards alike.

In fact, all four Vilcabamba rulers perished due to the Spanish, either directly or indirectly. Manco Inca was assassinated by Spaniards who had sought refuge in Vilcabamba, and who supposed that by killing the *sapa* Inca they could curry favour with the Spanish vice-regal authorities. Sayri Túpac was in all likelihood poisoned in Cuzco; Titu Cusi Yupanqui succumbed to pneumonia, a disease introduced to the Andes by the Spanish; and Túpac Amaru was executed. With his death and that of Carlos Melchor Inca in 1610, the title of *sapa* Inca fell into disuse, and royal survivors – of which there were many – assumed the role of local nobles and chiefs of various localities, gradually fading into the background of an increasingly Creole Spanish colony. Even so, the Inca ideal did not fade away, and by the end of the sixteenth century it had morphed into the *Incarrí* myth, a millennialist quasi-Arthurian legend in which it was said that Atahualpa's decapitated body would regrow its head, come back to life and set about re-establishing the Inca Empire.

Even though this was just an exercise in nostalgic hyperbole, the idea of a returning Inca would have more real offshoots than any other similar revivalist issue in South America. And they were not long in coming. First to the post was Pedro Bohórquez (1602– 1667), otherwise known as the False Inca, a Spaniard of Moorish ancestry who arrived in South America and took on the title of Inca Hualpa, supposedly a lost descendant of Huayna Cápac. His assumed heritage was taken up by the Calchaquí tribes of north-western Argentina in their pitiless but doomed struggle against the Spanish. Whether the Calchaquí tribes ever truly believed that he was a descendant of the Inca is lost to history, but he was set up as the titular head of the revolt against Spanish presence in this area, and was seen by the latter as a credible threat. Defeated and captured, his fate was to end in a Lima gaol before being garrotted in 1667 and his head set on a spike. The salient point from this episode is that even among non-Inca ethnic groups, such as the Calchaquí, where the empire maintained a looser, less direct form of control, the Inca ideal was still powerful enough to unite these often disparate and warring communities.

Of much greater import were a string of rebellions among indigenous groups during the late eighteenth century. These struck at the indigenous heart of the Andes in what is now highland Peru and Bolivia, and came close to subverting the then-existing Spanish-Creole order. Here leaders such as Túpac Catari (1750–1781) in Bolivia and José Gabriel Túpac Amaru (1738–1781) in Peru attempted to wrestle their respective lands from Spanish control. Their aim was to secure independent indigenous kingdoms. Both rebel leaders, and others such as Tomás Catari (1741–1781) and Diego Cristóbal Condorcanqui Castro Túpac Amaru (1750–1783), among others, harked back to the empire, seeing themselves as new Incas laying claim to that enduring legacy in their aim of establishing new indigenous states. Indeed, José Gabriel Túpac Amaru, born José Gabriel Condorcanqui Noguera, styled himself Túpac Amaru II, directly referencing the last doomed Vilcabamba *sapa* Inca, Túpac Amaru, who had been executed over two hundred years earlier in Cuzco. In fact, José Gabriel Túpac Amaru claimed to be a direct descendant of Túpac Amaru himself and, through him, of Huayna Cápac, the last undisputed Inca before the coming of the Spanish. Although these rebellions failed, they did foreshadow a weakening of Spanish colonial power, which was to be exploited by the same Creole elites that had defeated these indigenous uprisings only a generation earlier in the establishment of the various independent republics of South America.

As a final parenthesis on this theme, somewhat bizarrely, a number of the most august leaders of Argentine independence, Manuel Belgrano (1770–1820), José de San Martin (1778–1850) and Martín Miguel de Güemes (1785–1821), proposed the so-called Inca Plan at the Congress of Tucumán (1816), which aimed to restore an Inca as a constitutional monarch in Cuzco from which a proposed United Provinces of South America (later known as the United Provinces of the Río de la Plata) would be governed. The aim was to take power away from the burgeoning metropolis of Buenos Aires and legitimize the fledgling states of South America by installing a king, in this case an Inca one. Given the propensity for monarchical rule in Europe it was felt that a fellow monarch would be more readily accepted than a republic by the powers that be. Two candidates were considered: Colonel Dionisio Ucchu Inca Yupanqui y Bernal (b. 1760), a direct descendant of Pachacutec Inca Yupanqui on his mothers' side, and Juan Bautista Tupamaro (1747–1827), half-brother of the eighteenth-century Inca rebel Túpac Amaru II (1738–1781). In the end, resistance and obfuscation by Buenos Aires scuppered this plan. Nevertheless, it is yet another mark of the Inca's enduring appeal that all these numerous rebellions and plans harked back to the figurehead of the Cuzco monarch. As an afterthought, perhaps a token of that Inca Plan can still be glimpsed in the Argentine national flag with the Sun at its centre. This Sun, referred to as *Inti*, the Quechua name for that celestial body, makes an overt allusion to the Inca deity.

The publication of William Hickling Prescott's *History of the Conquest of Peru* in 1847 revived international interest in the Inca, as did the memoirs of numerous travellers to the Andes, such as E. G. Squier (1821–1888), J. J. von Tschudi (1818–1889) and Antonio Raimondi (1824–1890), among many others. All reflected a nostalgia for this lost world that was made more palpable to late nineteenth- and twentieth-century political thought through comparison of Inca statecraft to that of a paternalistic proto-socialist state by the likes of Heinrich Cunow (1862–1936) and Louis Baudin (1887–1964). By then archaeological expeditions to South America had revealed the uniqueness and sophistication of the Inca Empire and its predecessors in the Andes. This Inca world came to life in photos, especially those of the Peruvian Martín Chambi (1891–1973), who strove to capture the essence of an Andean way of life – that essential *lo Andino* as labelled by various anthropologists – seemingly unperturbed by modernity. His numerous photos of archaeological, especially Inca, ruins serve to frame his portraits of indigenous people and through these portraits one is offered a glimpse of the long past of Andean civilization.

Yet these paeans to a supposedly simpler, better past could not hide the fact that the indigenous population of the Andes was, and in many ways still is, more often than not a downtrodden, ostracized and vilified substratum of the modern societies they inhabit.

Martín Chambi, *Indian Varayoc and Family, Tinta Kanchis*, 1934, gelatin silver print (printed 1978).

This led to Peruvian political philosopher José Carlos Mariátegui's (1894–1930) musings on what he termed the 'Indian Question', in his seminal *Seven Interpretative Essays on Peruvian Reality*. The root of this question, for him, lay in the still existing, unequal, feudal, economic inequity, especially of lands, which followed the founding of Spanish colonial society in the sixteenth century. Even though Mariátegui did not mince his words concerning the indigenous population or the Incas, it is not hard to see where his sympathies lay, even promoting the Andean community known as the *ayllu* as the ideal and most logical institution for Peru to rebuild itself around during the Republican era. Mariátegui's take on Marxism adapted to the Peruvian, or South American, reality was a clarion call that was heeded later in the century by the revolutionary movements of the 1980s. It also served as the intellectual inspiration for the presidencies of Evo Morales in Bolivia (2006–19), Ollanta Humala in Peru (2011–16) and Rafael Correa in Ecuador (2007–17).

In Peru, the serial inequity and inequality in land distribution among the indigenous population led eventually to the only left-wing dictatorship in recent South American history, that of Juan Francisco Velasco Alvarado (1910–1977). His military dictatorship, which outlasted him by three years (1968–80), initiated a wide-ranging agrarian reform that raised and then dashed over four hundred years of pent-up indigenous hopes and aspirations, leading invariably to the rise of a new wave of revolutionary fervour and agitation. While the Maoist Shining Path will always be firmly associated with the violence of the 1980s and '90s, it is important to highlight the actions of the Guevarista revolutionary groups such as the Túpac Amaru Revolutionary Movement (MRTA) between 1982 and 1997 in Peru, and the Ejército Guerrillero Túpac Katari (EGTK, 1986–92) of Bolivia. In throwbacks to the last Vilcabamba *sapa* Inca, and the *nom de guerre* of his eighteenth-century successors, both the MRTA and the EGTK sought to better the plight of the ordinary Peruvians and Bolivians, especially those of the disempowered indigenous communities of the hinterland.

Although all these movements ultimately failed, there is nowadays a steadily growing pride and revindication of an indigenous – and in many regions an Inca – past among the native populations of the Andes, a past which is constantly being reassessed and assimilated into their struggles for rights and recognition. A major part of this revindication is rooted in a newfound pride in Quechua as the supposed language of the Inca, and its association to the modern Peruvian state. Similarly, Aymara is heralded for its assumed connections to Middle Horizon Tiahuanaco and is seen by some as directly linking this culture to the people, their language and onwards to modern Bolivia. This revalidation of Inca-ness can be seen from the ethno-nationalist ideology of the Peruvian Nationalist Party to a renaissance in Inca religion and festivities such as veneration of the *Pachamama* and the *Inti Raymi* and *Capac Raymi* solstice celebrations. Nor is the latter mere idle touristic posturing; rather, it is a rebirth of a too-long-buried identity. Yes, this identity has changed over the centuries – no identity can stay static if it wishes to survive – and perhaps it is not as 'pure' as some foreign tourists seeking a deeper truth might wish, but it is ultimately both authentic and modern.

In this way, and in many other subtle ways, the Inca are still alive and with us in the present day. So, going back to the original question at the start of this book, are the Inca truly a lost civilization? Well yes, but it is more complex than that, and I hope this book has in some measure addressed and given shape and substance to that inherent complexity.

Full bibliographical citations for the texts mentioned here can be found in the Bibliography.

The study of the Inca has excited popular and scholarly interest ever since European landfall and the conquest of the *Kingdom of Birú* or *Pirú* (as it was known to the early Spanish conquistadors) by Francisco Pizarro and his erstwhile companions in the 1530s. This means that the corpus of Inca books is extremely large, and still growing. Nevertheless, it is possible to winnow this down to a number of important texts for those interested in delving deeper into the world of the Inca.

In this sense, among the early tracts a number stand out due to their attention to detail and the quality of the material presented, some of it based on interviews with then-surviving indigenous witnesses. Of these, Juan de Betanzos's *Narrative of the Incas*, and Sarmiento de Gamboa's *History of the Incas*, are very interesting, given that they take, respectively, a more pro-Inca and pro-Spanish perspective on the proceedings. While Betanzos, married to an Inca princess, exalts the Inca and their style of government, Sarmiento, sponsored by the newly established Spanish viceroyalty, is at pains to show that the Inca Empire was a usurpers' realm and, as such, held little or no legitimacy in the Andes – in turn justifying Spanish takeover. Among these early texts, that by Titu Cusi Yupanqui (*History of How the Spaniards Arrived in Peru*), grandson of the eleventh and last undisputed Inca, Huayna Cápac, is perhaps the most interesting, providing a wholly indigenous perspective on the arrival of the Spanish and their conquest of the empire.

Slightly later come the first important texts by indigenous or *mestizo* writers. Of these, two are particularly exemplary: Inga Garcilaso de la Vega's *The Royal Commentaries of the Incas*, and Felipe Guaman Poma de Ayala's *Nueva Corónica y Buen Gobierno*. The latter is especially informative due to its stylized two-dimensional drawings of life under the Inca and the early Spanish colony, as well as its use of a florid hybrid Spanish–Quechua language as text. Dating to this late seventeenth century period are also Bernabé Cobo's two volumes on Inca religion, customs and history of the empire. Cobo's books borrow heavily from then-existing texts, including Polo de Ondegardo's lost book on Inca religion, and is an indispensable introduction into the intricacies of the empire as understood by the Spanish during the early colonial period.

Possibly the best modern recompilation of Inca imperial history based on ethnohistoric sources is María Rostworowski's splendid turn of the twenty-first century *History of the Inca Realm*. Her book makes important reading into the duality at the heart of Andean society and Inca kingship, while expanding on the little-known aspect of *yanacona* lords. That said, it is her interpretation of the foundational matrilineal nature of the *panacas* which is the real standout. This is a theme that is developed by other authors, although none more so than Francisco Hernández Astete in his brilliant *Los Incas y el poder de sus ancestros*. Both authors attest to the power and influence of women in the the Andean past. In this sense, the best concise, yet lucid, volume on the role of women in the Inca Empire, also by Francisco Hernández Astete, is *La mujer en el Tahuantinsuyo*. It reveals the power and agency of women in the Andes and within the Inca state, especially that of principal wives, or *coyas*.

More academic modern texts on the Inca also exist, among which is the sublime and simply entitled *The Incas*, by Terry D'Altroy, now in its second iteration. It is by far the most comprehensive, scholarly single volume on the Inca Empire out there, and a must for anyone wishing to expand their knowledge at a more academic level. An interesting companion volume to D'Altroy's book is Gary Urton and Adriana von Hagen's *Encyclopedia of the Incas*, which showcases concise essays on a variety of themes and topics by today's foremost Inca historians and archaeologists. For those wishing to delve into past Inca studies, perusing the giants of Andean studies, such as Wendell C. Bennett and Junius B. Bird's *Andean Culture History* or Philip Ainsworth Means's *Ancient Civilizations of the Andes*, is a must. Specific to the Inca themselves is John H. Rowe's insightful *An Introduction to the Archaeology of Cuzco*.

A more historical take on the Incas, and their demise in particular, is found in the still brilliant and eminently readable *The Conquest of the Incas* by John Hemming. This book was the first modern take on the collapse of the Inca since William Hickling Prescott's equally magnificent nineteenth-century *History of the Conquest of Peru*, written very much in the tradition of Edward Gibbon's *Rise and Fall of the Roman Empire*. John Hemming's seminal text uses many historical texts that had only come to light after Prescott's own book. In turn, Hemming's book has only recently been eclipsed by Alan Covey's *Inca Apocalypse*. This is a theme that is also addressed by Franklin G. Pease and his *Los Ultimos Incas del Cuzco*.

Turning to Inca specifics, the long article by John H. Rowe written in 1946 entitled 'Inca Culture at the Time of the Spanish Conquest' remains a classic, succinctly distilling a large amount of ethnohistoric information. For a recent take it is worthwhile consulting Martti Pärssinen's *Tawantinsuyu: El Estado Inca y Su Organización Política*. A closer perspective on the development of Cuzco and the rise of the Incas is to be had from Brian S. Bauer's *Ancient Cuzco*, while his volume entitled *The Sacred Landscape of the Inca* doubles up with Tom Zuidema's *The Ceque System of Cuzco* to explain the intricacies of shrine worship and ritual pilgrimage in the immediacies of Cuzco.

Inca religion, and especially the centrality of *huacas* to Andean cosmology, is also explored in Marco Curatola Petrocchi and Mariusz S. Ziółkowski's edited volume entitled *Adivinación y oraculos en el mundo andino antiguo*, and in Tamara Bray's edited volume *The Archaeology of Wak'as*. The denouement of Andean belief systems is scrutinized by Sabine MacCormack in her *Religion in the Andes: Vision and Imagination in Early Colonial Peru*, and from a Cuzco (and Lima) perspective by Gabriela Ramos in *Death and Conversion in the Andes: Lima and Cuzco, 1532–1670*. The role of the human *capacocha* in Inca ritual practice is dealt with in greater detail by Thomas Besom in his *Of Summits and Sacrifice*, and in Johan Reinhard and María Constanza Ceruti's *Inca Rituals and Sacred Mountains*, although the brevity and lucidity of Pierre Duviol's eponymous 1976 article still makes it a must-read.

Returning to Cuzco, Ian S. Farrington has written in *Cusco: Urbanism and Archaeology in the Inka World* the definite volume on the Incas' ancient capital. In the 1970s Graziano Gasparini and Luise Margolies wrote *Arquitectura Inka*, which was subsequently translated into English. Its treatment of Inca architecture has endured the test of time, supported by more specific studies such as *Inca Architecture and Construction at Ollantaytambo*, by Jean-Pierre Protzen, and Stella Nair's *At Home with the Sapa Inca: Architecture, Space, and Legacy at Chinchero*. Equally, John Hyslop's *The Inka Road System* and *Inka Settlement Planning* remain to this day the go-to volumes on these particular themes. Likewise, Terry LeVine's *Inka Storage Systems* is still a benchmark study on this topic.

Inca provincial life has been the subject of numerous works, although an edited volume by Michael A. Malpass and another one by the same author in conjunction with Sonia Alconini, entitled, respectively, *Provincial Inca* and *Distant Provinces in the Inka Empire*, provide an excellent introduction to this subject. A veritable page-turner on provincial life under the early Spanish colony can be found in Steve J. Stern's *Peru's Indian Peoples and the Challenge of Spanish Conquest: Huamanga to 1640*, while Noble David Cook remains the authority on how disease and epidemics ravaged the New World in his *Born to Die: Disease and New World Conquest, 1492–1650*. The financial running of the Inca Empire is best explained in Terry D'Altroy's article 'Funding the Inca Empire', found in Izumi Shimada's excellent edited volume simply named *The Inka Empire*. A detailed examination of the role of specialists or *camayocs* in the empire can be found in Julian Yates's article on the matter in the *Journal of Historical Geography*.

Inca suspension bridges are given a detailed overview in Brian S. Bauer's important 2006 article on the topic, found in *Andean Archaeology III*, edited by William H. Isbell and Helaine Silverman, while Gary Urton's *Inka History in Knots* provides the latest state-of-the-art treatise on the subject of *quipu*, the Inca knots-on-string 'writing' system. This book distils the results of years of research by the Harvard Khipu Database Project, especially the work of scholars such as Carrie Brezine and colleagues. In a similar vein, Frank Salomon's *The Cord Keepers* brings *quipu* studies up to the present day.

The complex issue of the timing of Inca expansion has yet to be the subject of a book, although John H. Rowe's original views on the issue and his short chronology for the rise of empire can be found in his seminal 1945 article 'Absolute Chronology in the Andean Area'. A cogent and robust defence of Rowe's Inca chronology from the perspective of Huayna Cápac's reign can be found in Susan Niles's excellent *The Shape of Inca History*. Pushback in the form of a longer timeline for expansion has recently been the subject of a number of articles in peer-reviewed journals; two in particular are worth mentioning: Dennis E. Ogburn's 'Reconceiving the Chronology of the Inca Imperial Expansion' and Erik Marsh et al., 'Dating the Expansion of the Inca Empire'. It is interesting to note the similarities the conclusions to these two articles bear with what Philip Ainsworth Means originally proposed regarding Inca expansion in his 1931 book.

For a modern assessment of the development of the Inca state, two articles stand out. The first, by Brian Bauer and Alan Covey, entitled 'The Development of the Inca State (AD 1000–1400)', provides a broad brush treatment to the eventual rise of the Inca, while Steve Kosiba's 'The Politics of Locality: Pre-Inka Social Landscapes of the Cusco Region' makes a fascinating case for how the intricacies of localism led to a commonly shared set of social and physical norms that opened the route to subsequent Inca consolidation.

The convoluted case for Inca rulership has been undertaken by many eminent scholars such as Tom Zuidema, Pierre Duviols, John Rowe, Peter Gose, Catherine Julien, Kerstin Nowack, María Rostworowski, Franklin Pease, Martti Pärssinnen and, recently, Shinya Watanabe. In these the orthodox view of a single-ruler monarchy has been posited by the likes of Gose, Julien and Rowe, while the various non-orthodox views – diarchy and triarchy – have been presented by Duviols, Nowack, Pease, Rostworowski and Zuidema, and Pärssinnen and Watanabe, respectively. In this case, it is interesting to note that it has mainly been North American researchers at the forefront of expounding the orthodox view (Gose, Julien, Rowe), while academics from other countries (Duviols, French; Nowack, German; Rostworowski and Pease, Peruvian; Zuidema, Dutch; Pärssinnen, Finnish; Watanabe, Japanese) have been more willing to interpret the available evidence in a different light.

While the ethnohistoric evidence is often contradictory and hard to disentangle, the fact that North American scholars tend to expound one view speaks volumes about how research and interpretation have been traditionally constituted, especially in as young a subject as Andean archaeology. In North America, and especially the United States, there has been a propensity towards the creation of hegemonic interpretative schools and narratives. In this case John H. Rowe and John V. Murra (with his *Vertical Archipelago* concept), among others, have cast a long shadow, and through their adherents they have dominated certain discourses within Andean archaeology to the present day. As with the discussion on the chronology of Inca Imperial expansion, it has often been hard to go against these dominant paradigms.

Outside of North America, the Andean archaeological scene has been much more fragmented and eclectic. While this has been construed as a weakness at the moment of establishing interpretations on various Andean themes, it has also meant that more often than not it has been more radical and willing to engage with a diverse range of models and concepts given its unfettered relationship with the dominant orthodoxy. We should caution, nevertheless, that this does not mean that they have not got it wrong in the past. On this theme, including the enduring controversy over whether the Inca was a unitary monarchy, diarchy or something even more complex, the best recent summary of all the different positions on this argument is Shinya Watanabe's *Estructura en los Andes Antiguos*. It provides an excellent introduction to this complex, though enthralling, subject.

Perhaps the best account of the horrors of Spanish (and Republican) colonial and post-colonial exploitation of Latin America can be found in Eduardo Galeano's visceral *Open Veins of Latin America*. Finally, on the perseverance and enduring nature of Andean culture, *The Hold that Life Has* by Catherine Allen is hard to beat, although there are numerous other excellent ethnographies by the likes of Thomas Abercombie, Inge Bolin and Penny Dransart, among many others. Finally, Francisco Ferreira and Billie Jean Isbell's edited volume *A Return to the Village* examines Andean culture in the present day, looking at how modernity and globalization have impacted on Andean village life. It is an excellent volume.

BIBLIOGRAPHY

Abercrombie, Thomas A., *Pathways of Memory and Power: Ethnography and History Among an Andean People* (Madison, WI, 1998)

Adamska, Anna, and Adam Mickczynski, 'Towards Radiocarbon Chronology of the Inca State', *Boletín de la Misión Arqueológica Andina*, 1 (1996), pp. 35–58

Adelaar, William F. H., *The Languages of the Andes* (Cambridge, 2004)

Alcock, Susan E., Terence N. D'Altroy, Kathleen D. Morrison and Carla M. Sinopoli, *Empires: Perspectives from Archaeology and History* (New York, 2001)

Allen, Catherine J., *The Hold Life Has: Coca and Cultural Identity in an Andean Community*, 2nd edn (Washington, DC, and London, 2002)

Arce Sotelo, Manuel, 'Yakumama, serenas y otras divinidades acuáticas del valle del Pampamarca (Ayacucho)', *Cuadernos Interculturales*, V/8 (2007), pp. 97–119

Arkush, Elizabeth, *Hillforts of the Ancient Andes: Colla Warfare, Society, and Landscape* (Gainesville, FL, 2011)

Astuhuamán, César, 'Los otros Pariacaca: oráculos, montañas y parentelas sagradas', in *Adivinación y oraculos en el mundo andino antiguo*, ed. Marco Curatola Petrocchi and Mariusz S. Ziółkowski (Lima, 2008), pp. 97–119

Bakewell, Peter, *Miners of the Red Mountain: Indian Labor in Potosi, 1545–1650* (Albuquerque, NM, 2010)

Baudin, Louis, *A Socialist Empire: The Incas of Peru* (Princeton, NJ, 1961)

Bauer, Brian S., *The Sacred Landscape of the Inca: The Cusco Ceque System* (Austin, TX, 1998)

—, 'The Early Ceramics of the Inca Heartland', *Fieldiana*, 31 (1999), pp. 1–156

—, *Ancient Cuzco: The Heartland of the Inca*, Joe R. and Teresa Long Series in Latin American and Latino Art and Culture (Austin, TX, 2004)

—, 'Suspension Bridges of the Inca Empire', in *Andean Archaeology*, vol. III: *North and South*, ed. William H. Isbell and Helaine Silverman (New York, 2006), pp. 468–93

—, and Wilton Barrionuevo Orosco, 'Reconstructing Andean Shrine Systems: A Text Case from the Xaquixaguana (Anta) Region of Cusco, Peru', *Andean Past*, V/8 (1998), pp. 73–87

—, and R. Alan Covey, 'The Development of the Inca State (AD 1000–1400)',
in *Ancient Cuzco: Heartland of the Inca*, ed. Brian S. Bauer (Austin, TX,
2004), pp. 71–90

—, and Lucas C. Kellett, 'Cultural Transformations of the Chanka Homeland
(Andahuaylas, Peru) during the Late Intermediate Period (AD 1000–
1400)', *Latin American Antiquity*, XXI/1 (2010), pp. 87–111

—, Lucas C. Kellett and Miriam Aráoz Silva, *The Chanka: Archaeological
Research in Andahuaylas (Apurimac), Peru* (Los Angeles, CA, 2010)

—, and Charles Stanish, *Ritual and Pilgrimage in the Ancient Andes: The Islands
of the Sun and the Moon* (Austin, TX, 2001)

Bennett, Wendell C., 'Chimu Archeology', *Scientific Monthly*, XLV/1 (1937),
pp. 35–48

—, *Excavations at Wari, Ayacucho, Peru* (New Haven, CT, 1953)

—, and Junius B. Bird, *Andean Culture History*, 2nd edn (New York, 1960)

Bernand, Carmen, *The Incas: People of the Sun* (New York, 1994)

Besom, Thomas, *Of Summits and Sacrifice: An Ethnohistoric Study of Inka
Religious Practices* (Austin, TX, 2009)

Betanzos, Juan de, *Narrative of the Incas* (Austin, TX, 1996)

Binford, Lewis R., 'Archaeology as Anthropology', *American Antiquity*,
XXVIII/2 (1962), pp. 217–25

Bird-David, Nurit, 'Animism Revisited: Personhood, Environment, and
Relational Epistemology', *Current Anthropology*, XL (1999), pp. 67–91

Bolin, Inge, *Rituals of Respect: The Secret of Survival in the High Peruvian Andes*
(Austin, TX, 1998)

Bray, Tamara L., ed., *The Archaeology of Wak'as: Explorations of the Sacred in
the Pre-Columbian Andes* (Boulder, CO, 2015)

Brezine, Carrie, 'Algorithms and Automation: The Production of Mathematics
and Textiles', in *The Oxford Handbook of the History of Mathematics*, ed.
Eleanor Robson and Jacqueline Stedall (New York, 2008), pp. 468–94

Brown, Kendall W., 'Workers' Health and Colonial Mercury Mining at
Huancavelica, Peru', *The Americas*, LVII/4 (2001), pp. 467–96

Butzer, Karl W., 'Cattle and Sheep from Old to New Spain: Historical
Antecedents', *Annals of the Association of American Geographers*, LXXVIII/1
(1988), pp. 29–56

Cobo, Bernabé, *History of the Inca Empire* (Austin, TX, 1979)

—, *Inca Religion and Customs* (Austin, TX, 1990)

Conrad, Geoffrey W., and Arthur A. Demarest, *Religion and Empire: The
Dynamics of Aztec and Inca Expansionism* (Cambridge, 1984)

Cook, Noble David, *Demographic Collapse: Indian Peru, 1520–1620*
(Cambridge, 1981)

—, *Born to Die: Disease and New World Conquest, 1492–1650* (Cambridge, 1998)

Cornejo, Luis, 'Sobre la cronología del inicio de la imposición cuzqueña en
Chile', *Estudios Atacameños*, 47 (2014), pp. 101–16

Costin, Cathy, 'Housewives, Chosen Women, Skilled Men: Cloth Production and Social Identity in the Late Pre-Hispanic Andes', *Archaeological Papers of the American Anthropological Association*, 8 (1998), pp. 123–41

Covey, R. Alan, 'Chronology, Succession, and Sovereignty: The Politics of Inka Historiography and its Modern Interpretation', *Comparative Studies in Society and History*, XLVIII/1 (2006), pp. 169–99

—, *Inca Apocalypse: The Spanish Conquest and the Transformation of the Andean World* (Oxford, 2020)

Cunow, Heinrich, *Geschichte Und Kultur Des Inkareiches. Ein Beitrag Zur Kulturgeschichte Altamerikas* (Amsterdam, 1937)

Curatola Petrocchi, Marco, and Mariusz S. Ziółkowski, eds, *Adivinación y oraculos en el mundo andino antiguo* (Lima, 2008)

D'Altroy, Terence N., *Provincial Power in the Inca Empire* (Washington, DC, 1992)

—, 'Remaking the Social Landscape: Colonization in the Inka Empire', in *The Archaeology of Colonial Encounters: Comparative Perspectives*, ed. Gil J. Stein (Santa Fe, NM, 2005), pp. 263–96

—, *The Incas*, 2nd edn (Oxford, 2014)

—, 'Funding the Inca Empire', in *The Inka Empire: A Multidisciplinary Approach*, ed. Izumi Shimada (Austin, TX, 2014), pp. 97–120

—, and Timothy Earle, 'Staple Finance, Wealth Finance, and Storage in the Inka Political Economy (with Comment)', *Current Anthropology*, XXVI/2 (1985), pp. 187–206

—, Veronica I. Williams, and Ana Maria Lorandi, 'The Inkas in the Southlands', in *Variations in the Expression of Inka Power*, ed. Richard L. Burger, Craig Morris and Ramiro Matos Mendieta (Washington, DC, 2007), pp. 85–133

Delaere, Christophe, José M. Capriles and Charles Stanish, 'Underwater Ritual Offerings in the Island of the Sun and the Formation of the Tiwanaku State', *PNAS*, CXVI/17 (2019), pp. 8233–8

Denevan, William M., *Cultivated Landscapes of Native Amazonia and the Andes* (Oxford, 2001)

Demarest, A., *Viracocha: The Nature and Antiquity of the Andean High God* (Cambridge, MA, 1981)

Dillehay, Tom D., *The Settlement of the Americas: A New Prehistory* (New York, 2001)

—, Herbert H. Eling Jr and Jack Rossen, 'Preceramic Irrigation Canals in the Peruvian Andes', *PNAS*, CII/47 (2005), pp. 17241–4

Donkin, Robin Arthur, *Agricultural Terracing in the Aboriginal New World* (Tucson, AZ, 1979)

Dransart, Penny Z., *Earth, Water, Fleece and Fabric: An Ethnography and Archaeology of Andean Camelid Herding* (London, 2002)

Duviols, Pierre, 'La capacocha: mecanismo y función del sacrificio humano, su proyección, su papel en la política integracionista y en la economía redistributiva del Tawantinsuyu', *Allpanchis Phuturinqa*, IX (1976), pp. 11–57

—, 'La dinastia de los Incas: Monarquia or Diarquia? Argumentos heuristicos a favor dc una tcsis cstructuralista', *Journal de la société des américanistes*, CXVI (1979), pp. 67–83

Eeckhout, Peter, ed., *Arqueología de la costa central del Perú en los periodos tardíos* (Lima, 2004)

Farrington, Ian S., 'The Archaeology of Irrigation Canals, with Special Reference to Peru', *World Archaeology*, XI/3 (1980), pp. 287–305

—, *Cusco: Urbanism and Archaeology in the Inka World* (Gainesville, FL, 2013)

Ferreira, Francisco, and Billie Jean Isbell, eds, *A Return to the Village: Community Ethnographies and the Study of Andean Culture in Retrospective* (London, 2016)

Galeano, Eduardo, *Open Veins of Latin America: Five Centuries of the Pillage of a Continent* (New York, 1997)

Gasparini, Graziano, and Luise Margolies, *Arquitectura Inka* (Caracas, 1977)

Glowacki, Mary, 'Food of the Gods or Mere Mortals? Hallucinogenic Spondylus and Its Interpretive Implications for Early Andean Society', *Antiquity*, 79 (2005) pp. 257–68

Godoy, R., *Mining and Agriculture in Highland Bolivia: Ecology, History, and Commerce among the Jukumanis* (Tucson, AZ, 1990)

Gose, Peter, 'The Past Is a Lower Moiety: Diarchy, History, and Divine Kingship in the Inka Empire', *History and Anthropology*, IX/4 (1996), pp. 383–414

Gramsci, Antonio, *The Modern Prince and Other Writings* (New York, 1957)

Grobman, Alexander, et al., 'Preceramic Maize from Paredones and Huaca Prieta, Peru', *PNAS*, CIX/5 (2012), pp. 1755–9

Guaman Poma de Ayala, Felipe, *Nueva corónica y buen gobierno* (Lima, 1993)

Guthrie, Stewart Elliott, *Faces in the Clouds: A New Theory of Religion* (Oxford, 1993)

Harlan, Jack R., 'Agricultural Origins: Centers and Noncenters', *Science*, CLIV/4008 (1971), pp. 468–74

Hastorf, Christine A., 'The Effect of the Inka State on Sausa Agricultural Production and Crop Consumption', *American Antiquity*, LV/2 (1990), pp. 262–90

Hemming, John, *The Conquest of the Incas* (London, 1970)

Hernández Astete, Francisco, *La mujer en el Tahuantinsuyo* (Lima, 2002)

—, 'Las panacas y el poder en el Tahuantinsuyo', in *Dinámicas del poder: historia y actualidad de la autoridad andina*, ed. Chantal Caillavet and Susan Elizabeth Ramírez (Lima, 2008), pp. 29–45

—, *Los Incas y el poder de sus ancestros* (Lima, 2012)

Hyland, Sabine, 'Writing with Twisted Cords: The Inscriptive Capacity of Andean *Khipus*', *Current Anthropology*, 58 (2017), pp. 412–19

Hyslop, John, *The Inka Road System* (Orlando, FL, and London, 1984)
—, *Inka Settlement Planning* (Austin, TX, 1990)
Ioannidis, Alexander G., et al., 'Native American Gene Flow into Polynesia Predating Easter Island Settlement', *Nature*, 583 (2020), pp. 572–7
Isbell, William H., and Gordon F. McEwan, eds, *Huari Administrative Structure: Prehistoric Monumental Architecture and State Governement* (Washington, DC, 1991)
Julien, Catherine J., *Reading Inca History* (Iowa City, IA, 1990)
Kamen, Henry, *Spain, 1469–1714: A Society of Conflict* (London, 2014)
Kolata, Alan L., *The Tiwanaku* (Oxford, 1993)
—, *Ancient Inca* (Cambridge, 2013)
Kosiba, Steve, 'The Politics of Locality: Pre-Inka Social Landscapes of the Cusco Region', in *The Archaeology of Politics: The Materiality of Political Practice in the Past*, ed. P. Johansen and A. Bauer (Newcastle, 2011), pp. 114–50
Kus, James S., 'The Chicama-Moche Canal: Failure or Success? An Alternative Explanation for an Incomplete Canal', *American Antiquity*, XLIX/2 (1984), pp. 408–15
Lane, Kevin, 'Through the Looking Glass: Re-assessing the Role of Agro-pastoralism in the North-central Andean Highlands', *World Archaeology*, XXXVIII/3 (2006), pp. 493–510
—, and Gabriela Contreras Ampuero, 'An Inka Administrative Site in the Ancash Highlands, North-central Andes', *Past*, 56 (2007), pp. 13–15
—, Oliver Huaman, Luis Coll, Alexander G. Pullen, David Beresford-Jones and Charles French, 'De fronteras y enclaves: la presencia Nasca en la sierra de Ica (260 a.C. – 640 d.C.)', *Boletín de Arqueología PUCP*, 22 (2017), pp. 117–32
Lapolla, Alberto J., 'La Patria Grande Perdida: El Congreso de Tucumán y El proyecto del Rey Inca de Belgrano, San Martín y Güemes', 2005, www.elhistoriador.com
Letchman, Heather, 'Technologies of Power: The Andean Case', in *Configurations of Power: Holistic Anthropology in Theory and Practice*, ed. Patricia J. Netherley (Ithaca, NY, 1993), pp. 244–80
LeVine, Terry Y., *Inka Storage Systems* (Norman, OK, 1992)
Lindo, John, Randall Haas, et al., 'The Genetic Prehistory of the Andean Highlands 7000 years BP though European Contact', *Science Advances*, IV/11 (2018)
Lopes Machado, C., 'Cronología del Estado Inca', *Estudios Atacameños*, 18 (1999), pp. 133–40
MacCormack, Sabine, *Religion in the Andes: Vision and Imagination in Early Colonial Peru* (Princeton, NJ, 1993)
—, '¿Inca o Español? Las identidades de Paullu Topa Inca', *Boletin de Arqueologia PUCP*, 8 (2004), pp. 99–109
MacQuarrie, Kim, *The Last Days of the Incas* (New York, 2008)

Malpass, Michael A., *Provincial Inca: Archaeological and Ethnohistorical Assessment of the Impact of the Inca State* (Iowa City, IA, 1993)

—, 'Variability in the Inca State: Embracing a Wider Perspective', in *Provincial Inca: Archaeological and Ethnohistorical Identification of the Impact of the Inca State*, ed. Michael A. Malpass (Iowa City, IA, 1993), pp. 234–44

—, and Sonia Alconini, *Distant Provinces in the Inka Empire: Toward a Deeper Understanding of Inka Imperialism* (Iowa City, IA, 2010)

Marsh, Erik J., Ray Kidd, Dennis Ogburn and Víctor Durán, 'Dating the Expansion of the Inca Empire: Bayesian Models from Ecuador and Argentina', *Radiocarbon*, LIX/1 (2017), pp. 117–40

Maza, Jesús, 'Introducción al estudio arqueológico del canal prehispánico Huiru Catac, cuenca alta de Nepeña: Tecnología Hidráulica para integrar la puna, los valles interandinos y la costa', *Arkinka*, 265 (2017), pp. 78–87

Means, Philip Ainsworth, *Ancient Civilizations of the Andes* (New York and London, 1931)

Medinaceli, Ximena, 'Paullu y Manco ¿una Diarquía Inca En Tiempos de Conquista?', *Bulletin de l'Institut Français d'Etudes Andines*, 36 (2007), pp. 241–58

Medrano, Manny, and Gary Urton, 'Toward the Decipherment of a Set of Mid-colonial Khipus from the Santa Valley, Coastal Peru', *Ethnohistory*, 65 (2018), pp. 1–23

Mengoni, Guillermo L., and Hugo D. Yacobaccio, 'The Domestication of South American Camelids: A View from the South-central Andes', in *Documenting Domestication: New Genetic and Archaeological Paradigms*, ed. Melinda A. Zeder, Daniel G. Bradley, Eve Emshwiller and Bruce D. Smith (Berkeley, CA, 2006), pp. 228–44

Moore, Jerry D., and Carol J. Mackey, 'The Chimú Empire', in *Handbook of South American Archaeology*, ed. Helaine Silverman and William H. Isbell (New York, 2008), pp. 783–808

Morris, Craig, 'Inka Strategies of Incorporation and Governance', in *Archaic States*, ed. Gary M. Feinman and Joyce Marcus (Santa Fe, NM, 1998), pp. 293–310

Moscovich, Viviana, *El Khipu y la yupana: administración y contabilidad en el Imperio Inca* (Arequipa, 2016)

Moseley, Michael, *The Maritime Foundations of Andean Civilization* (Menlo Park, CA, 1975)

Murra, John V., 'Herds and Herders in the Inca State', in *Man, Culture and Animals: The Role of Animals in Human Ecological Adjustments*, ed. Anthony Leeds and Andrew P. Vayda (Washington, DC, 1965), pp. 185–215

—, 'An Aymara Kingdom in 1567', *Ethnohistory*, XV/2 (1968), pp. 115–51

—, *La organización económica del estado Inca* (Mexico City, 1978)

—, '"El Archipélago Vertical" Revisited', in *Andean Ecology and Civilization: An Interdisciplinary Perspective on Andean Ecological Complementarity*, ed. S. Masuda, I. Shimada and C. Morris (Tokyo, 1985), pp. 3–14

—, 'The Limits and Limitiations of the "Vertical Archipelago" in the Andes',
in *Andean Ecology and Civilization: An Interdisciplinary Perspective on
Andean Ecological Complementarity*, ed. S. Masuda, I. Shimada and
C. Morris (Tokyo, 1985), pp. 15–20

—, 'Cloth, Textile, and the Inca Empire', in *The Peru Reader*, ed. Orin Starn, Iván
Degregori and Robin Kirk, 2nd edn (Durham, 2005), pp. 55–69

Nair, Stella, *At Home with the Sapa Inca: Architecture, Space, and Legacy at
Chinchero* (Austin, TX, 2015)

Nickel, Cheryl, 'The Semiotics of Andean Terracing', *Art Journal*, XLII/3 (1982),
pp. 200–203

Niles, Susan, *The Shape of Inca History: Narrative and Architecture in an
Andean Empire* (Iowa City, IA, 1999)

Nowack, Kerstin, *Ceque and More: A Critical Assessment of R. Tom Zuidema's
Studies on the Inca* (Bonn, 1998)

Ochsendorf, John, 'Engineering Analysis for Construction History:
Opportunities and Perils', *Second International Congress on Construction
History* (2006), pp. 89–107

Ogburn, Dennis E., 'Dynamic Display, Propaganda, and the Reinforcement
of Provincial Power in the Inca Empire', *Archaeological Papers of the
American Anthropological Association*, XIV/1 (2004), pp. 225–39

—, 'Reconceiving the Chronology of the Inca Imperial Expansion',
Radiocarbon, LIV/4 (2012), pp. 219–37

Ortloff, Charles R., *Water Engineering in the Ancient World: Archaeological and
Climate Perspectives on Societies of Ancient South America, the Middle East
and South-east Asia* (Oxford, 2010)

—, Michael E. Moseley and Robert A. Feldman, 'Hydraulic Engineering
Aspects of the Chimu Chicama-Moche Intervalley Canal', *American
Antiquity*, XLVII/4 (1982), pp. 572–95

Pardo Grau, Cecilia, and Gary Urton, eds, *Khipus* (Lima, 2020)

Park, C. C., 'Water Resources and Irrigation Agriculture in Pre-Hispanic Peru',
Geographical Journal, CXLIX/2 (1983), pp. 153–66

Pärsinnen, Martti, *Tawantinsuyu: El estado inca y su organización política*
(Lima, 2003)

—, 'Collasuyu of the Inka State', in *The Inka Empire: A Multidisciplinary
Approach*, ed. Izumi Shimada (Austin, TX, 2015), pp. 265–86

Pease, Franklin G. Y., *Los últimos incas del Cuzco* (Lima, 2004)

Perri, Angela, et al., 'New Evidence of the Earliest Domestic Dogs in the
Americas', *American Antiquity*, LXXXIV (2019), pp. 68–87

Pickersgill, Barbara, 'Domestication of Plants in the Americas: Insights from
Mendelian and Molecular Genetics', *Annals of Botany*, C/5 (2007), pp. 925–40

Potter, Ben A., et al., 'Current Evidence Allows Multiple Models for the
Peopling of the Americas', *Science Advances*, 4 (2018)

Prescott, William Hickling, *History of the Conquest of Peru* (New York, 1847)

Prieto, Gabriel, et al., 'A Mass Sacrifice of Children and Camelids at the Huanchaquito-Las Llamas Site, Moche Valley, Peru', PLOS One, 14 (2019)

Protzen, Jean-Pierre, *Inca Architecture and Construction at Ollantaytambo* (Oxford, 1993)

Pulgar Vidal, Javier, *Geografía del Perú: Las ocho regiones naturales* (Lima, 1967)

Quesada, Marcos N., 'El diseño de las redes de riego y las escalas sociales de la producción agrícola en el 1er milenio DC (Tebenquiche Chico, Puna de Atacama)', *Estudios Atacameños*, 31 (2006), pp. 31–46

Raimondi, Antonio, *Colección Estudios Geológicos y Mineros Para La Obra 'El Perú': El Departamento de Ancachs* (Lima, 2006)

Ramírez, Susan Elizabeth, 'Negociando el Imperio: El estado Inca como culto', in *Dinámicas del poder: historia y actualidad de la autoridad andina*, ed. Chantal Caillavet and Susan Elizabeth Ramírez (Lima, 2008), pp. 5–18

Ramos, Gabriela, *Death and Conversion in the Andes: Lima and Cuzco, 1532–1670* (Notre Dame, IN, 2010)

Reinhard, Johan, and María Constanza Ceruti, *Inca Rituals and Sacred Mountains: A Study of the World's Highest Archaeological Sites* (Los Angeles, CA, 2010)

Rostworowski, María, *Estructuras andinas del poder: Ideología religiosa y política* (Lima, 1983)

—, *Conflicts over Coca Fields in XVIth-century Peru* (Ann Arbor, MI, 1988)

—, *Costa Peruana Prehispánica* (Lima, 1989)

—, 'Breve Ensayo sobre el Señorío de Ychma', in *Costa Peruana Prehispánica*, ed. M. Rostworowski (Lima, 1989), pp. 71–8

—, *History of the Inca Realm* (Cambridge, 1999)

—, and Pilar Remy, *Las Visitas a Cajamarca 1571–72/1578: Documentos* (Lima, 1985)

Rowe, John H., *An Introduction to the Archaeology of Cuzco* (Cambridge, MA, 1944)

—, 'Absolute Chronology in the Andean Area', *American Antiquity*, X/3 (1945), pp. 265–84

—, 'Inca Culture at the Time of the Spanish Conquest', in *Handbook of South American Indians*, ed. Julian H. Steward (Washington, DC, 1946), pp. 183–330

—, 'Archaeological Explorations in Southern Peru, 1954–1955', *American Antiquity*, XXII/2 (1956), pp. 135–51

—, 'Stages and Periods in Archaeological Interpretation', *Southwest Journal of Anthropology*, 18 (1962), pp. 40–54

—, 'La Constitucion Inca Del Cuzco', *Histórica*, IX/1 (1985), pp. 35–73.

—, 'La Supuesta "Diarquia" de Los Incas', *Reviste Del Instituto Americano de Arte Del Cusco*, 14 (1994), pp. 99–107

Salomon, Frank, '"The Beautiful Grandparents": Andean Ancestor Shrines and Mortuary Ritual as Seen Through Colonial Records', in *Tombs for the*

Living: Andean Mortuary Practices, ed. Tom D. Dillehay (Washington, DC, 1995), pp. 315–53

—, *The Cord Keepers: Khipus and Cultural Life in a Peruvian Village* (Durham, 2004)

—, Carrie Brezine, Gino de las Casas and Víctor Falcón, 'Los khipus de Rapaz en casa: un complejo administrativo-ceremonial centroperuano', *Revista andina*, 43 (2006), pp. 59–92

—, and Stuart B. Schwartz, eds, *The Cambridge History of the Native Peoples of the Americas* (Cambridge, 1999)

Sancho de la Hoz, Pedro, *Relación de La Conquista Del Perú* (New York, 1917)

Sandoval, José R., et al., 'Genetic Ancestry of Families of Putative Inka Descent', *Molecular Genetics and Genomics*, 293 (2018), pp. 873–81

Santa Cruz Pachacuti Yamqui, Joan, *Relación de antiguedades deste reyno del Pirú* (Lima and Cusco, 1993)

Sarmiento de Gamboa, Pedro, *History of the Incas* (London, 1999)

Scarborough, Vernon L., *The Flow of Power: Ancient Water Systems and Landscapes* (Santa Fe, NM, 2003)

Schroedl, Annette, 'La Capacocha Como Ritual Político: Negociaciones en torno al poder entre Cuzco y los curacas', in *Dinámicas del poder: historia y actualidad de la autoridad andina*, ed. Chantal Caillavet and Susan Elizabeth Ramírez (Lima, 2008), pp. 19–27

Seaman, Rebecca M., *Conflict in the Early Americas: An Encyclopedia of the Spanish Empire's Aztec, Incan, and Mayan Conquests* (Santa Barbara, CA, 2013)

Shimada, Izumi, ed., *The Inka Empire: A Multidisciplinary Approach* (Austin, TX, 2015)

Silverman, Helaine, and William H. Isbell, eds, *Handbook of South American Archaeology* (New York, 2008)

Squier, Ephraim George, *Peru: Incidents and Explorations in the Land of the Incas* (New York, 1877)

Stern, Steve J., *Peru's Indian Peoples and the Challenge of Spanish Conquest: Huamanga to 1640*, 2nd edn (Madison, WI, 1993)

Taylor, Gerald, 'Camac, Camay y Camasca en el manuscrito quechua de Huarochirí', in *Camac, Camay y Camasca*, ed. Gerald Taylor (Lima, 2000), pp. 1–19

Treacy, John M., and William M. Denevan, 'The Creation of Cultivated Land through Terracing', in *The Archaeology of Garden and Field*, ed. Naomi F. Miller and Kathryn L. Gleason (Philadelphia, PA, 1994), pp. 91–110

Trigger, Bruce G., 'Monumental Architecture: A Thermodynamic Explanation of Symbolic Behaviour', *World Archaeology*, XXII/2 (1990), pp. 119–32

Tschudi, Johann Jakob von, *Reise Durch Südamerika* (Leipzig, 1866)

Tylor, E. B., *Primitive culture: Religion in Primitive Culture* (New York, 1958)

Unamuno, Miguel de, *En Torno al Casticismo* (Madrid and Barcelona, 1866)

Urton, Gary, *At the Crossroads of Earth and Sky: An Andean Cosmology* (Austin, TX, 1988)

—, *The History of a Myth: Paqaritambo and the Origin of the Inkas* (Austin, TX, 1990)

—, *Inca Myths* (Austin, TX, 1999)

—, *Inka History in Knots: Reading Khipus as Primary Sources* (Austin, TX, 2017)

—, and Carrie J. Brezine, 'Khipu Typologies', in *Their Way of Writing: Scripts, Signs, and Pictographics in Pre-Columbian America*, ed. E. H. Boone and Gary Urton (Washington, DC, 2011), pp. 319–52

—, and Adriana von Hagen, eds, *Encyclopedia of the Incas* (Lanham, MY, 2015)

Vasquez de Espinoza, Antonio, *Compendium and Description of the West Indies* (Washington, DC, 1942)

Vega, Garcilaso de la, *The Incas: The Royal Commentaries of the Incas* (Lima, 1979)

Vega-Centeno, Rafael, 'Economías Tardías: Producción y Distribución En Los Andes Centrales Antes y Durante La Expansión Del Tawantinsuyu (900–1532 d.C.)', in *Historia económica del antiguo Perú*, ed. Peter Kaulicke, Hugo C. Ikehara, Rafael Segura Llanos and Rafael Vega-Centeno (Lima, 2019), pp. 403–533

Villegas Páucar, Samuel, '¿Indio o Criollo? Identidad Etnica Del Diputado Dionisio Inca Yupanqui En Las Cortes de Cadiz', *Nueva Corónica* (2013), vol. I, pp. 1–10

Vivanco Pomacanchari, Cirilo, 'Obras Hidráulicas de Etapa Prehispánica En Huaccana, Chincheros – Apurímac', *Arqueologia y Sociedad*, 30 (2015), pp. 315–33

Watanabe, Shinya, *Estructura en los Andes Antiguos* (Yokohama, 2013)

Yates, Julian S., 'Historicizing "Ethnodevelopment": Kamayoq and Political-economic Integration across Governance Regimes in the Peruvian Andes', *Journal of Historical Geography*, XLVI (2014), pp. 53–65

Yupanqui, Titu Cusi, *History of How the Spaniards Arrived in Peru* (Indianapolis, IN, and Cambridge, 2006)

Zuidema, R. Tom., *The Ceque System of Cuzco: The Social Organization of the Capital of the Inca* (Leiden, 1964)

—, 'Hierarchy and Space in Incaic Social Organization', *Ethnohistory*, XXX/2 (1983), pp. 49–75

—, 'Inca Religion: Its Foundations in the Central Andean Context', in *Native Religions and Cultures of Central and South America*, ed. Lawrence E. Sullivan (New York and London, 2002), pp. 236–53

ACKNOWLEDGEMENTS

The rather glib title which I coined for this speech a year ago – long before I started to give it any serious thought was 'Archaeology: Handmaiden to History.'

IVOR NOËL HUME, 1964

This book focuses on the causes and events behind the rise of the Incas, their collapse and what remained afterwards. I can truly say that it has been an enjoyable experience. However, this task would have been impossible without the support and encouragement of certain individuals, among them Brian Reyes, Tim Mohr and Andrew Canessa. Veronica Grant, a retired teacher from La Cumbre, Argentina, and one-time volunteer archaeologist on my excavation, served as copy-editor for a substantial chunk of this book. Jennifer Grant, Alex Herrera, Jean-Paul Latin and Erik Marsh helped to edit individual chapters, their contribution in this regard was equally invaluable. Luis Coll was responsible for all the maps and plans in this book. At Reaktion Books I am grateful to Ben Hayes, who commissioned me to write this book, and to Michael Leaman for keeping tabs on me until I did. Amy Salter has been a joy to work with and an excellent editor throughout this process, while Alex Ciobanu was a guiding light during the fraught process of selecting images for this volume. Thanks also go to Phoebe Colley, who did a terrific job at copy-editing this manuscript, and to out-of-house book designer Simon Buchanan, who set out this beautiful tome. I just hope my text does all your combined efforts justice.

The measured comments of Frank Meddens made the final text that much more cogent; I am grateful to him, especially to his assiduous search for passages in Spanish chronicles alluding to the 'metal-eating' capabilities of Spanish horses and their effect on the indigenous population's imagination. I also thank Veronica Williams and Erik Marsh for their invaluable advice on the themes of *mitmas* and Inca chronology, respectively. My eternal gratitude to the other two Cambridge Andean musketeers, Alex Herrera and David Beresford-Jones. Both have been inestimable field companions and our wide-ranging conversations on Andean archaeology have always been a major source of insight and inspiration. As sounding boards for ideas, themes and concepts, they both have few equals. In this remit I must also include George Lau: assured and dispassionate, his advice was always welcomed. In Peru I thank Mario Advincula and Oliver Huaman Oros, whose ever fruitful conversations on Inca archaeology have been a font of knowledge. Back in the UK, I thank Elizabeth DeMarrais, my erstwhile PhD supervisor, who instilled in me a love for archaeological theory.

A number of themes in this book, especially in Chapters Two, Six and Seven, were initially developed during an Alexander von Humboldt Fellowship at the Freie Universität Berlin in 2011–12, under the inspired mentorship of Michael Meyer. My gratitude goes to him for the trust he placed in me. Chapter Three expands on ideas first mooted in a separate article published in Tim Insoll's *Oxford Handbook of the Archaeology of Ritual and Religion* (2011).

My wife and archaeologist fellow-traveller, Jennifer Grant, was also a constant source of encouragement and ideas. I thank Thomas (Tommy), my son, for his patience. My eternal gratitude to the Lazarus Group – you know who you are – your irony, cynicism and constant hectoring about my fascination with 'small walls' have always forced me to keep it real. Finally, my gratitude to Los Belking's, Françoise Hardy, Los Shain's, The Showmen, Zouzou and the whole gamut of Peruvian and French New Wave, as well as Northern Soul, which were my musical companions along the way.

The author and publishers wish to express their thanks to the below sources of illustrative material and/or permission to reproduce it. Some locations of artworks are also given below, in the interest of brevity:

Biblioteca Nacional del Perú, Lima: p. 161; Brooklyn Museum, NY: pp. 75, 142, 143; The Cleveland Museum of Art, OH: p. 86; courtesy Luis Coll: pp. 18, 22, 56, 57, 80; photo courtesy Jennifer Grant: p. 109 (top); photo courtesy Oliver Huaman Oros: p. 94; Det Kongelige Bibliotek, Copenhagen (GKS 2232 4°): pp. 85, 90, 159; photos Kevin Lane: pp. 37, 50 (bottom), 66 (bottom), 76, 82, 92, 95, 97, 98 (bottom), 105, 106, 109 (top), 152; © 2022 Martín Chambi Archive/digital image © 2022 The Museum of Modern Art/Scala, Florence: p. 176; The Metropolitan Museum of Art, New York: pp. 6, 49; Q?rius, The Coralyn W. Whitney Science Education Center, National Museum of Natural History, Smithsonian Institution, Washington, DC: p. 102; photo courtesy Bill Sillar: p. 50 (top); Wiktor Szymanowicz/Alamy Stock Photo: p. 170; Victoria and Albert Museum, London: p. 162; Christian Vinces/ Shutterstock.com: p. 31; The Walters Art Museum, Baltimore, MD: p. 34.

Jimmy Harris, the copyright holder of the image on p. 68, and Beatrice Murch (blmurch), the copyright holder of the image on p. 15, have published them online under conditions imposed by a Creative Commons Attribution 2.0 Generic License. Bill Simon, the copyright holder of the image on p. 111 (top), has published it online under conditions imposed by a Creative Commons Attribution-ShareAlike 2.0 Generic License. Brooklyn Museum, the copyright holder of the images on pp. 66 (top) and 89, has published them online under conditions imposed by a Creative Commons Attribution 3.0 Unported License. Bernard Gagnon, the copyright holder of the image on p. 33; Paradais Sphynx (Manu10), the copyright holder of the image on p. 108; Martin St-Amant, the copyright holder of the image on pp. 98–9; Stevage, the copyright holder of the image on p. 81; and Kyle Thayer, the copyright holder of the image on pp. 26–7, have published them online under conditions imposed by a Creative Commons Attribution-ShareAlike 3.0 Unported License. Diego Delso (delso.photo), the copyright holder of the images on pp. 14 and 154–5; Thomas Fuhrmann (SnowmanStudios), the copyright holder of the image on p. 111 (bottom); and Aga Khan (IT), the copyright holder of the image on p. 83, have published them online under conditions imposed by a Creative Commons Attribution-ShareAlike 4.0 International License. Readers are free to: share — copy and redistribute the material in any medium or format; adapt — remix, transform, and build upon the material for any purpose, even commercially. Under the following terms:

Page numbers in *italics* refer to illustrations